D1546714

CONTENTS

INTRODUCTION

I have been a Vegan all through my life and am proud of that. My Mom and Dad were full plant based vegans. Veganism is more than just a meal plan, it is a lifestyle which helps you live a healthy life. It helps to reduce your chances of suffering chronic ill health conditions like: obesity, high cholesterol, high blood pressure, heart diseases, type II diabetes, stroke etc.

Meats are not the only source of protein, there are tons of delicious plant sources of protein which are richer and healthier than meat. Weight loss is assured when you cook plant based foods in your air fryer. It ensures that you stay away from those unhealthy fats. You also enjoy Guilt-free meals.

Whether you are new to Veganism and Vegetarian lifestyle, this Essential Vegan & Vegetarian Cookbook is a sure guide. You will learn 800 new vegan and vegetarian air fryer recipes of different categories, from keto to weight loss, with nutritional info per serving. You will also enjoy a 40 Day Vegan and Vegetarian meal prep diet plan with your air fryer. The cookbook has 5 sections. Below is the summary of the sections of this cookbook:

- **Section 1:** Healthy Vegan and Vegetarian Air Fryer Weight Loss Recipes
- **Section 2:** Vegan and Vegetarian Air Fryer Low Fat Recipes
- **Section 3:** Plant Based Vegans and Vegetarians Air Fryer Weight Loss Recipes
- **Section 4:** Vegans and Vegetarians Air Fryer Recipes for Special Seasons
- **Section 5:** 40 Days Air Fryer Meal Prep Recipes for Vegans and Vegetarians

Follow the recipe guides in this cookbook and spice up your Vegan and Vegetarian lifestyle!

VEGAN TIPS FOR BEGINNERS

Veganism is more than a lifestyle. It is an ideal feeding style recommended for everybody especially those who suffer from obesity, high cholesterol and high blood pressure, heart diseases, type II diabetes, stroke etc.

For those who are new in the world of veganism, **"A vegan does not consume any animal product - no egg, no dairy products, and no meat of any kind."** Many vegans also avoid honey and some even do not use or wear products made with animal fur, skin, bones, etc. Also, Vegans love and protect animals. Most Vegan diet followers are actually looked upon as radical animal rights activists. There are many vegan substitutes for eggs and dairy products.

Healthy vegans eat a wide variety of foods to ensure they get all the necessary nutrients that their body needs, such as vitamin B-12, iron and proteins. There are many sources of these nutrients in the vegan diet, so it is just a myth that vegans tend to suffer nutritional deficiencies. Vegan diet has tremendous health benefits as well. Not only can it prevent diseases such as cancer, type II diabetes, arthritis, osteoporosis, obesity, heart diseases, etc.

Health Benefits Of Veganism

- Vegan dieters have significantly lower BMI compared to their omnivorous counterparts.
- Vegan diet can improve cardiovascular health as it is significantly lower in saturated fats.
- The high fiber content of the vegan diet can lower the risk of colon cancer.
- The diet is great for bone health, as it is high in Magnesium, which aids in better absorption of calcium.
- Vegan dieters look younger and prevent premature aging, thanks to the high antioxidant content of the diet.
- Vegan diets are high in potassium which is crucial for having a healthy heart.
- The alkaline content of fruits and vegetables reduces inflammation caused by acidic diets. This prevents pain in the joints and other areas of the body.
- The detoxifying effects of the diet can be seen in the form of improved health of the kidney.
- The high levels of vitamins C in the diet boost immunity to prevent chronic conditions and seasonal disorders. It is also of great benefit to the gums.
- The diet does not contain cholesterol that is normally available in meat-based and dairy-rich diets.
- Research reveals that vegan diets prevent and even reverse cancers.
- Veganism is known to cause some relief from chronic conditions like migraines.
- Vegan diet is known to benefit the overall health of the skin, nails and hair, since the diet is rich in fruits and vegetables containing antioxidants.
- Bad breath and body odor can be eliminated by avoiding animal protein intake.
- Nuts, seeds and vegetables can benefit the skin and the complexion.
- Eliminating refined foods, sugars and unhealthy fats along with dairy and meat products can lead to lower BMI and reduced obesity.

Some Common Vegan Kitchen Condiments

Here are some of the common vegan ingredients that should be available in the kitchen of a Vegan. I will be using these ingredients in the recipes of this cookbook.

- Seitan - chewy protein rich food which is an ideal meat substitute

- Baking Powder
- Baking Soda
- Dried Fruits - Medjool dates, apricots, plums, raisins, peaches, apples
- Apple Sauce
- Nut Butter – can be made at home using peanuts, almonds, cashews, etc. You can also buy vegan butter readymade.
- Tahini Sauce
- Low Sodium Soy Sauce
- Chili Sauce
- Snacks - sesame sticks, granola, cereal bar, crackers, vegan cookies like trail mix cookies
- Mustard
- Ketchup
- Vegan Mayo
- Whole Grains - quinoa, barley, wheat bran
- Assortment of Nuts - cashews, walnuts, Macadamia nuts, Brazil nuts, hazel nuts, peanuts, pecans
- Assortment of Seeds - chia, flax, hemp, sunflower, safflower, pumpkin, Sesame (white or black)
- Oils - coconut, olive, canola, flaxseed, and vegetable oil, as well as oils for salads like walnut oil.
- Sweeteners - maple syrup, agave nectar, stevia
- Vinegars - rice, white, apple cider, balsamic
- Blackstrap Molasses (extremely rich in calcium and iron)
- Citrus Fruits - lemons, limes, oranges, tangerines, grapefruit
- Sea Salt and Rock Salt
- Dried and Canned Beans - all varieties like pinto, lima beans, cannellini, refried beans, lentils, chickpeas, red beans, and etc.
- Tomatoes - fresh, canned, paste, diced, sauce, whole, or sundried
- Pumpkin - fresh or canned
- Canned Artichokes
- Coconut Milk
- Garlics - all varieties
- Onions - all varieties
- Potatoes - all varieties
- Rice - brown or white
- Pasta - whole wheat
- Oats - steel cut or rolled
- Nutritional Yeast
- Pepper
- Low Sodium Seasonings (Mrs. Dash brand name is recommended)
- Vegetable Broth
- Mushrooms - fresh, dried, or canned
- Vanilla Extracts

- Dried Herbs and Spices - ginger powder or root, garlic powder, onion powder, turmeric, curry power, thyme, rosemary, lemongrass, basil, dill, oregano, rosemary, Coriander, cumin, cinnamon, bay leaf, sage, cardamom, red pepper flakes
- Flours - refined wheat flour, whole wheat flour, rye, arrowroot powder, rice flour, chickpea or garbanzo flour (available in most Asian grocery stores), corn meal, corn starch, corn flour, potato starch, potato flour, buckwheat, amaranth flour, sorghum flour
- Fresh Fruits - apples, pears, bananas, cantaloupes, melons, berries, peaches, plums, watermelon, avocado, etc.
- Fresh Veggies - bok choy, cabbage, cauliflower, broccoli, Brussels Sprouts, egg plants, artichokes, asparagus, fennel, spinach, Swiss chard, kale, arugula, carrots, celery, string beans, root vegetables, lettuce, pumpkin, sweet potatoes, peas.
- Breads and Tortillas
- Tofu and Tempeh
- Vegan Cheese
- Miso
- Non Dairy Milk - rice milk, soy milk, almond milk
- Freezer Items - frozen fruits like bananas, berries, frozen veggies, non-dairy ice cream, etc.

HOW TO CLEAN YOUR AIR FRYER

Cleaning your air fryer after every use is very important. It keeps your appliance in tip-top shape and functioning properly. It also keeps any foul smell away and prevents residue build-up. More importantly, when your air fryer is clean, you are sure that the food you are preparing is clean and safe to eat.

For the Basket and Drawer:

1.   Put the air fryer basket in the container with warm soapy water. Let soak in the solution for at least 10 minutes.

2.   With a scrubber or a sponge, scrub ant dirt off from the basket – use a delicate, non-abrasive scrub/sponge that will not harm the basket in any way.

3.   When all the dirt is scrubbed off, rinse the basket under running tap water. Repeat the process with the drawer.

4.   NEVER use an abrasive material to clean it. Otherwise, you will damage the drawer.

For the Housing:

1.   The housing will not become as greasy as the basket and the drawer, so cleaning will not be too difficult. However, still need to clean it regularly.

2.   Use a moist, soft cloth to wipe off dirt and grease from the outside of the housing.

3.   Use hot water and a soft sponge to clean the inner surfaces of the housing.

4.   Use a soft-medium bristle brush to clean the heating element, especially if some food residues that stick to it.

5.   Wipe it dry with paper towels. NEVER use an abrasive brush or a steel brush to clean it. Otherwise, you will damage the heating element.

For the Coil:

You should clean the coil of your air fryer every 3 months. If you notice that smoke is coming out of the vent of your air fryer, then you should also clean it. If you use your air fryer to cook a lot, then you should clean the coil at least once a month.

1.   Unplug the air fryer and let cool completely.

2.   Carefully turn the air fryer upside down.

3.   Using a moist tissue, wipe any dirt from the coil and then using a soft-bristled brush, clean it thoroughly.

4.   When the coil is clean, dry it using a clean towel.

5.   Carefully turn the air fryer to its right position.

What If My Air Fryer Is Very Dirty?

1.   Dissolve 3 grams of baking powder for every100 milliliters of water in a spray bottle.

2.   Remove the drawer and basket from the housing and clean them as instructed above.

3.   Carefully turn the air fryer upside down. Shake the bottle with the cleaning solution until well mixed.

4.   Spray the solution around the heater area. Let the solution soak for a couple of minutes.

5.   Carefully turn the air fryer to its right position. Let it stand for 30 minutes.

6.   Carefully turn the air fryer upside down again.

7.   Shake the bottle with the cleaning solution until well mixed.

8.   Spray the solution around the heater area. Let the solution soak for a couple of minutes.

9.   Carefully turn the air fryer to its right position. Let it stand for 30 minutes.

10.   Return the drawer to the housing. Pour about 400 milliliters water into the drawer.

11.   Plug the air fryer and set the timer for 20 minutes at the lowest temperature – this will moisten any dirt and lodge them off.

12.   The drawer will catch them as they fall. Pull the drawer open and remove.

13.   Unplug the air fryer and let cool enough to handle and clean.

14.   Carefully turn the air fryer upside down.

15.   Using a paper towel or a clean cloth, wipe the cleaning solution and the softened dirt from the surface. Wipe clean the rest of the inside surface.

16.   Clean the drawer and dry. Assemble the basket back into the drawer, and return the drawer back into the housing.

A clean air fryer is a healthy air fryer, so keep your appliance clean as much as possible. Remember to clean with utmost precaution and care.

SOME COOKING TERMINOLOGIES

These are some of the cooking terms I will be using from time to time. It is good to familiarize yourself with these terminologies now. I also included some measurements. I may not have used all these terms in this book because I listed them before I started writing the manuscript.

Beat: To use a spoon, a fork, a whisk, or an electric mixer to mix ingredients together, using a fast circular movement

Blend: To combine two or more ingredients until the mixture is smooth and uniform in texture, color, and flavor

Bread: To coat a food in bread crumbs before frying or baking

Chill: To put the food in the refrigerator for at least 2 hours

Chop: To cut into little pieces

Combine: To put items together or place them in the same bowl

Dice: To cut into small square pieces

Drain: To remove all the liquid—may be done in a colander, strainer or by pressing a plate against the food while tilting the container forward

Fold: To gently combine a light, delicate substance (such as beaten egg whites) with a heavier mixture, using a light "over-and–under" motion

Grate: To scrape against the small holes of a grater, making thin little pieces

Grease: To coat a pan with oil or margarine so food does not stick when cooking

Marinate: To soak foods in a flavorful liquid that tenderizes or adds flavor to meat, fish, chicken, veggies, or tofu

Mash: To squash food with a fork, spoon, or masher

Melt: To use heat to make a solid into a liquid

Mince: To cut into very small pieces, smaller than chopped or diced

Mix: To stir together with a spoon, fork, or electric mixer

Peel: To remove the outside of a fruit or vegetable

Pit: To remove the seed

Preheat: To turn your oven on ahead of time so it heats up to the temperature you need it to be before cooking

Shred: To scrape against the large holes on a grater, making long, thin pieces

Stir: To mix with a spoon

Strain: To remove solid bits from liquid

Wash: To clean thoroughly (Fresh fruits that do not have skins to peel and all fresh veggies need to be cleaned with a special brush before using.)

Whisk: To use a whisk to quickly stir to get lumps out

Bake: To cook in an oven

Boil: To heat on the stove until the liquid gets hot enough for bubbles to rise and break the surface

Broil: To cook by direct heat in the broiler of an electric or gas range

Brown: To cook until the color of the food changes to brown

Fry: To cook food in hot fat such as olive oil or butter ("deep fry" means to put enough fat in the pan to cover the food)

Roast: The same as bake, but this term is used with cooking meat

Sauté: To cook quickly in a little oil, butter, or margarine

Scramble: To mix up really well (to scramble eggs, stir while they cook)

Simmer: To cook in liquid over low heat just below the boiling point (bubbles form slowly and burst before reaching the surface)

Steam: To cook food using the heat from boiling water without putting the food directly in the water—usually done with a device called a steamer (a silver bowl with holes that folds to fit many different pans)

Stew: To cook food for a long time in a covered pan, with liquid

Stir-fry: To toss and stir cut-up pieces of food in a pan with hot oil, cooking it quickly

MEASUREMENTS AND CONVERSIONS

Units Abbreviations And Meanings

Dash = a small amount. A little less than a pinch.

Pinch = 1/8 teaspoon. Taking a little between your thumb and forefinger; a little more than a dash.

tsp. = teaspoon

tbsp. = tablespoon

Pkg. = package

oz. = ounce

Med. = medium

lb. = pound

Measurement Conversion Scales

Dash = 1/16 teaspoon

Pinch = ⅛ teaspoon

1 tablespoon = 3 teaspoons

1 cup = 16 tablespoons

1 cup = 8 ounces

1 pound = 16 ounces

1 pint = 2 cups

1 quart = 2 pints or 4 cups

1 gallon = 4 quarts or 16 cups

1 ml = ⅕ teaspoon

1 teaspoon = 5 ml

1 tablespoon = 15 ml

1 ounce = 30 ml

1 cup = 240 ml

1 ounce = 28 grams

1 pound = 454 grams

1 liter = 34 ounces

100 grams = 3.5 ounces

1 kilogram = 2.2 pounds

1 kilogram = 35 ounces

3 teaspoons = 1 tablespoon

4 tablespoons = 1/4 cup

16 tablespoons = 1 cup

1/4 cup + 1/4 cup = 1/2 cup

1/2 cup + 1/2 cup = 1 cup

1 cup = 8 ounces

1 pound = 16 ounces

2 cups = 1 pint = 16 ounces

2 pints = 1 quart = 32 ounces

2 quarts = 1/2 gallon = 64 ounces

SECTION 1: HEALTHY VEGAN AND VEGETARIAN AIR FRYER WEIGHT LOSS RECIPES

Potato Appetizer with Garlic-Mayo Sauce

Servings: 4
Total Time: 20 Minutes
Calories: 277
Fat: 50 g
Protein: 1.7 g
Carbs: 6 g
Fiber: 3 g
Ingredients and Quantity
- 2 tbsp. vegetable oil of your choice
- Kosher salt and freshly ground black pepper, to taste
- 3 Russet potatoes, cut into wedges

For the Dipping Sauce:
- 2 tsp. dried rosemary, crushed
- 3 garlic cloves, minced
- 1/3 tsp. dried marjoram, crushed
- 1/4 cup sour cream
- 1/3 cup mayonnaise

Direction
1. Lightly grease your potatoes with a thin layer of vegetable oil.
2. Season with salt and ground black pepper.
3. Arrange the seasoned potato wedges in an air fryer cooking basket.
4. Bake at 395 degrees F for 15 minutes, shaking once or twice.
5. In the meantime, prepare the dipping sauce by mixing all the sauce ingredients.
6. Serve the potatoes with the dipping sauce and enjoy!

Sweet Potato Fries

Servings: 4
Total Time: 20 Minutes
Calories: 180
Fat: 5.4 g
Protein: 1.8 g
Carbs: 31.8 g
Fiber: 1 g
Ingredients and Quantity
- 1 1/2 tbsp. olive oil
- 1/2 tsp. smoked cayenne pepper
- 3 sweet potatoes, peeled and cut into 1/4 inch long slices
- 1/2 tsp. shallot powder
- 1/3 tsp. freshly ground black pepper, or more, to taste
- 3/4 tsp. garlic salt

Direction
1. Firstly, preheat your air fryer to 360 F.
2. Then, add the sweet potatoes to a mixing dish; toss them with the other ingredients.
3. Cook the sweet potatoes approximately 14 minutes.
4. Serve with a dipping sauce of choice. Enjoy!

Spicy Cheesy Risotto Balls

Servings: 4
Total Time: 26 Minutes
Calories: 176
Fat: 9.1 g
Protein: 4.7 g
Carbs: 16.9 g
Fiber: 2 g

Ingredients and Quantity

- 3 oz. cooked rice
- 1/2 cup roasted vegetable stock
- 1 egg, beaten
- 1 cup white mushrooms, finely chopped
- 1/2 cup seasoned breadcrumbs
- 3 garlic cloves, peeled and minced
- 1/2 yellow onion, finely chopped
- 1/3 tsp. ground black pepper, or more, to taste
- 1 1/2 bell peppers, seeded, minced
- 1/2 chipotle pepper, seeded and minced
- 1/2 tbsp. Colby cheese, grated
- 1 1/2 tbsp. canola oil
- Sea salt, to savor

Direction

1. Heat a saucepan over a moderate heat; now, heat the oil and sweat the garlic, onions, bell pepper and chipotle pepper until tender.
2. Throw in the mushrooms and fry until they are fragrant and the liquid has almost evaporated.
3. Throw in the cooked rice and stock; boil for 18 minutes.
4. Now, add the cheese and spices; mix to combine.
5. Allow the mixture to cool completely.
6. Shape the risotto mixture into balls.
7. Dip the risotto balls in the beaten egg; then roll them over the breadcrumbs.
8. Air fry risotto balls for 6 minutes at 400 degrees F.
9. Serve with marinara sauce. Enjoy!

Easy Cheesy Broccoli

Servings: 4
Total Time: 25 Minutes
Calories: 103
Fat: 9.1 g
Protein: 1.9 g
Carbs: 4.9 g
Fiber: 1.2 g

Ingredients and Quantity

- 1/3 cup grated yellow cheese
- 1 large-sized head broccoli, stemmed and cut small florets
- 2 1/2 tbsp. canola oil
- 2 tsp. dried rosemary
- 2 tsp. dried basil
- Salt and ground black pepper, to taste

Direction

1. Bring a medium pan filled with a lightly salted water to a boil.
2. Then, boil the broccoli florets for about 3 minutes.
3. Then, drain the broccoli florets well; toss them with the canola oil, rosemary, basil, salt and black pepper.
4. Set your air fryer to 390 degrees F; arrange the seasoned broccoli in the cooking basket; set the timer for 17 minutes.
5. Toss the broccoli halfway through the cooking process.
6. Serve warm topped with grated cheese and enjoy!

Potato and Kale Croquettes

Servings: 6
Total Time: 10 Minutes
Calories: 309
Fat: 6.9 g
Protein: 12.1 g
Carbs: 49.8 g
Fiber: 2 g

Ingredients and Quantity
- 4 eggs, slightly beaten
- 1/3 cup flour
- 1/3 cup goat cheese, crumbled
- 1 1/2 tsp. fine sea salt
- 4 garlic cloves, minced
- 1 cup kale, steamed
- 1/3 cup breadcrumbs
- 1/3 tsp. red pepper flakes
- 3 potatoes, peeled and quartered
- 1/3 tsp. dried dill weed

Direction
1. Firstly, boil the potatoes in salted water.
2. Once the potatoes are cooked, mash them; add the kale, goat cheese, minced garlic, sea salt, red pepper flakes, dill and one egg; stir to combine well.
3. Now, roll the mixture to form small croquettes.
4. Grab three shallow bowls. Place the flour in the first shallow bowl.
5. Beat the remaining 3 eggs in the second bowl.
6. After that, throw the breadcrumbs into the third shallow bowl.
7. Dip each croquette in the flour; then, dip them in the eggs bowl; lastly, roll each croquette in the breadcrumbs.
8. Air fry at 335 degrees F for 7 minutes or until golden.
9. Taste, adjust for seasonings and serve warm. Enjoy!

Spicy Potato Wedges

Servings: 4
Total Time: 25 Minutes
Calories: 309
Fat: 4.7 g
Protein: 5.4 g
Carbs: 44.5 g
Fiber: 3.3 g

Ingredients and Quantity
- 1 1/2 tbsp. melted butter
- 1 tsp. dried parsley flakes
- 1 tsp. ground coriander
- 1 tsp. seasoned salt
- 3 large red potatoes, cut into wedges
- 1/2 tsp. chili powder
- 1/3 tsp. garlic pepper

Direction
1. Dump the potato wedges into the air fryer cooking basket.
2. Drizzle with melted butter and cook for 20 minutes at 380 degrees F. Make sure to shake them a couple of times during the cooking process.
3. Add the remaining ingredients; toss to coat potato wedges on all sides. Serve and enjoy!

Stuffed Mushrooms

Servings: 2
Total Time: 16 Minutes
Calories: 176
Fat: 14.7 g
Protein: 6 g
Carbs: 10.5 g
Fiber: 4 g

Ingredients and Quantity
- 2 tsp. cumin powder
- 4 garlic cloves, peeled and minced
- 1 small onion, peeled and chopped
- 2 tbsp. bran cereal, crushed
- 18 medium-sized white mushrooms
- Fine sea salt and freshly ground black pepper, to your taste
- A pinch ground allspice
- 2 tbsp. olive oil

Direction
1. First, clean the mushrooms; remove the middle stalks from the mushrooms to prepare the "shells".
2. Grab a mixing dish and thoroughly combine the remaining items.
3. Fill the mushrooms with the prepared mixture.
4. Cook the mushrooms at 345 degrees F heat for 12 minutes. Enjoy!

Mediterranean Halloumi and Garlic Omelet

Servings: 2
Total Time: 17 Minutes
Calories: 444
Fat: 29 g
Protein: 30 g
Carbs: 11.6 g
Fiber: 2 g

Ingredients and Quantity
- 1/3 cup Halloumi cheese, sliced
- 2 tsp. garlic paste
- 2 tsp. fresh chopped rosemary
- 5 well-whisked eggs
- 2 bell peppers, seeded and chopped
- 1 1/2 tbsp. fresh basil, chopped
- 3 tbsp. onions, chopped
- Fine sea salt and ground black pepper, to taste

Direction
1. Spritz your baking dish with a canola cooking spray.
2. Throw in all ingredients and stir until everything is well incorporated.
3. Bake for about 15 minutes at 325 degrees F.
4. Eat warm. Enjoy!

Mashed Ruby Yams

Servings: 4
Total Time: 20 Minutes
Calories: 223
Fat: 14.7 g
Protein: 4.8 g
Carbs: 18.6 g
Fiber: 5 g

Ingredients and Quantity

- 1/3 cup maple syrup
- 2 eggs, beaten
- 1/2 tsp. ground black pepper
- 1 tsp. cayenne pepper
- 1/3 cup extra virgin olive oil
- 1 1/2 tsp. pink Himalayan salt flakes
- 5 ruby yams, peeled
- 1 1/2 tbsp. heavy cream

Direction

1. Boil ruby yams until they're fork tender.
2. Then, combine all the remaining ingredients using an electric mixer or a wire whisk.
3. Scrape the mixture into a baking dish.
4. Transfer the baking dish to the air fryer and bake for 20 minutes at 305 degrees F. Serve and enjoy!

Mediterranean-Style Frittata with Manchego

Servings: 4
Total Time: 40 Minutes
Calories: 153
Fat: 11.9 g
Protein: 9.3 g
Carbs: 3.2 g
Fiber: 1.7 g

Ingredients and Quantity

- 1/3 cup grated Manchego cheese
- 5 eggs
- 1 small onion, finely chopped
- 2 garlic, peeled and finely minced
- 1 1/2 cups white mushrooms, chopped
- 1 tsp. dried basil
- 1 1/2 tbsp. olive oil
- 3/4 tsp. dried oregano
- 1/2 tsp. dried parsley flakes or 1 tbsp. fresh flat leaf Italian parsley
- 1 tsp. porcini powder
- Table salt and freshly ground black pepper, to savor

Direction

1. Start by preheating your air fryer to 350 degrees F.
2. Add the oil, mushrooms, onion, and green garlic to the air fryer baking dish.
3. Bake this mixture for 6 minutes or until it is tender.
4. Meanwhile, crack the eggs into a mixing bowl; beat the eggs until they're well whisked.
5. Next, add the seasonings and mix again.
6. Pause your air fryer and take the baking dish out of the air fryer.
7. Pour the whisked egg mixture into the baking dish with sautéed mixture.
8. Top with the grated Manchego.
9. Bake for about 32 minutes at 320 degrees F or until your frittata is set.
10. Serve warm garnished with diced fresh tomatoes. Enjoy!

Saucy Sweet Potatoes with Zucchini and Peppers

Servings: 4
Total Time: 20 Minutes
Calories: 225
Fat: 12.9 g
Protein: 2.8 g
Carbs: 27.3 g
Fiber: 4 g

Ingredients and Quantity

- 1/4 cup olive oil
- 1 Serrano pepper, deveined and thinly sliced
- 1 bell pepper, deveined and thinly sliced
- 2 large-sized sweet potatoes, peeled and quartered
- 1 to 2 carrots, cut into matchsticks
- 1 1/2 tbsp. maple syrup
- 1/2 tsp. porcini powder
- 1/4 tsp. mustard powder
- 1/2 tsp. fennel seeds
- 1 medium-sized zucchini, sliced
- 1 tbsp. garlic powder
- 1/4 tsp. ground black pepper
- 1/2 tsp. fine sea salt
- Tomato ketchup, for serving

Direction

1. Place the sweet potatoes, zucchini, peppers and the carrot into the air fryer cooking basket.
2. Drizzle with olive oil and toss to coat; cook in the preheated machine at 355 degrees F for 14 minutes.
3. While the vegetables are cooking, prepare the sauce by thoroughly whisking the other ingredients, without the tomato ketchup.
4. Lightly grease a baking dish that fits into your machine.
5. Transfer cooked vegetables to the prepared baking dish; add the sauce and toss to coat well.
6. Turn the machine to 395 degrees F and cook the vegetables for 4 more minutes.
7. Serve warm with tomato ketchup on the side. Enjoy!

Herbed Potatoes with Mediterranean Dipping Sauce

Servings: 4
Total Time: 20 Minutes
Calories: 303
Fat: 12.2 g
Protein: 8.5 g
Carbs: 37.3 g
Fiber: 3.1 g

Ingredients and Quantity

- 2 pounds Russet potatoes, peeled and cubed
- 1 1/2 tbsp. melted butter
- 1 tsp. sea salt flakes
- 1 sprig rosemary, leaves only, crushed
- 2 sprigs thyme, leaves only, crushed
- 1/2 tsp. freshly cracked black peppercorns
- For the Mediterranean Dipping Sauce:
- 1/2 cup mascarpone cheese
- 1/3 cup yogurt
- 1 tbsp. freshly dill, chopped
- 1 tbsp. olive oil

Direction

1. Firstly, set your Air Fryer to cook at 360 degrees F.
2. Now, add the potato cubes to the bowl with cold water and soak them approximately for 33 minutes.
3. After that, dry the potato cubes using a paper towel.
4. In a mixing dish, thoroughly whisk the melted butter with sea salt flakes, rosemary, thyme, and freshly cracked peppercorns.
5. Rub the potato cubes with this butter/spice mix.
6. Air-fry the potato cubes in the cooking basket for 17 to 20 minutes or until cooked through; make sure to shake the potatoes to cook them evenly.
7. Meanwhile, make the Mediterranean dipping sauce by mixing the remaining ingredients.
8. Serve warm potatoes with Mediterranean sauce for dipping. Enjoy!

Onion Rings with a Twist

Servings: 8
Total Time: 30 Minutes
Calories: 231
Fat: 3.3 g
Protein: 8.7 g
Carbs: 41.4 g
Fiber: 4.5 g

Ingredients and Quantity
- 1 1/4 cups seasoned breadcrumbs
- 2 cups flour
- 1/2 tsp. baking soda
- 1 tsp. baking powder
- 2 medium sized yellow onions, cut into rings
- 1 1/2 tsp. sea salt flakes
- 2 medium-sized eggs
- 1/2 tsp. green peppercorns, freshly cracked
- 1/2 tsp. dried dill weed
- 1/4 tsp. paprika
- 1 1/2 cup plain milk

Direction
1. Begin by preheating your Air Fryer to 350 degrees F.
2. Place the onion rings into a bowl with cold water; let them stay 16 to 20 minutes.
3. Drain the onion rings and pat them dry with a kitchen towel.
4. In a shallow bowl, mix the flour together with the baking powder, baking soda and sea salt flakes.
5. Then, coat each onion ring with the flour mixture.
6. In another bowl, beat the eggs with the milk; add the mixture to the remaining flour mixture and whisk well.
7. Place the onion rings into the batter.
8. In a third bowl, mix the green peppercorns, seasoned breadcrumbs, dill and paprika.
9. Roll the onion rings over the breadcrumb mix, covering well.
10. Air fry them in the cooking basket for 8 to 11 minutes or until thoroughly cooked golden. Serve and enjoy!

Roma Tomato Bites with Halloumi Cheese

Servings: 4
Total Time: 20 Minutes
Calories: 428
Fat: 38.4 g
Protein: 18.8 g
Carbs: 4.5 g
Fiber: 2.2 g

Ingredients and Quantity

For the Sauce:
- 1/3 cup extra-virgin olive oil
- 1/2 cup Parmigiano-Reggiano cheese, grated
- 1 tsp. garlic puree
- 1/2 tsp. fine sea salt
- 4 tbsp. pecans, chopped

For the Tomato Bites:
- 2 large sized Roma tomatoes, cut into thin slices and pat them dry
- 8 oz. Halloumi cheese, cut into thin slices
- 1 tsp. dried basil
- 1/4 tsp. red pepper flakes, crushed
- 1/8 tsp. sea salt
- 1/3 cup onions, sliced
- 1 tsp. dried basil

Direction

1. Start by preheating your air fryer to 380 F.
2. Make the sauce by mixing all ingredients, except the extra-virgin olive oil, in your food processor.
3. While the machine is running, slowly and gradually pour in the olive oil; puree until everything is well - blended.
4. Now, spread 1 teaspoon of the sauce over the top of each tomato slice.
5. Place a slice of Halloumi cheese on each tomato slice.
6. Top with onion slices. Sprinkle with basil, red pepper, and sea salt.
7. Transfer the bites to the Air Fryer basket.
8. Drizzle with olive oil and cook for approximately 14 minutes.
9. Arrange these bites on a nice serving platter, garnish with the remaining sauce and serve at room temperature. Enjoy!

Crispy Fried Pickle Spears

Servings: 6
Total Time: 15 Minutes
Calories: 58
Fat: 2 g
Protein: 3.2 g
Carbs: 6.8 g
Fiber: 1 g

Ingredients and Quantity
- 1/3 cup milk
- 1 tsp. garlic powder
- 2 medium-sized eggs
- 1 tsp. fine sea salt
- 1/3 tsp. chili powder
- 1/3 cup all-purpose flour
- 1/2 tsp. shallot powder
- 2 jar sweet and sour pickle spears

Direction
1. Pat the pickle spears dry with a kitchen towel.
2. Then, take two mixing bowls. Whisk the egg and milk in a bowl.
3. In another bowl, combine all dry ingredients.
4. Firstly, dip the pickle spears into the dry mix; then coat each pickle with the egg/milk mixture; dredge them in the flour mixture again for additional coating.
5. Air fry battered pickles for 15 minutes at 385 degrees. Enjoy!

Spicy Winter Squash Bites

Servings: 8
Total Time: 23 Minutes
Calories: 113
Fat: 3 g
Protein: 1.6 g
Carbs: 22.6 g
Fiber: 2 g

Ingredients and Quantity
- 2 tsp. fresh mint leaves, chopped
- 1/3 cup brown sugar
- 1 1/2 tsp. red pepper chili flakes
- 2 tbsp. melted butter
- 3 pounds winter squash, peeled, seeded and cubed

Direction
1. Toss all of the above ingredients in a large-sized mixing dish.
2. Roast the squash bites for 30 minutes at 325 degrees F in your Air Fryer, turning once or twice.
3. Serve with a homemade dipping sauce. Enjoy!

Butter Squash Fritters

Servings: 4
Total Time: 22 Minutes
Calories: 152
Fat: 10 g
Protein: 5.8 g
Carbs: 9.4 g
Fiber: 1.3 g

Ingredients and Quantity
- 1/3 cup all-purpose flour
- 1/3 tsp. freshly ground black pepper, or more, to taste
- 1/3 tsp. dried sage
- 4 garlic cloves, minced
- 1 1/2 tbsp. olive oil
- 1/3 butternut squash, peeled and grated
- 2 eggs, well whisked
- 1 tsp. fine sea salt
- A pinch ground allspice

Direction
1. Thoroughly combine all ingredients in a mixing bowl.
2. Preheat your air fryer to 345 degrees and set the timer for 17 minutes; cook until your fritters are browned.
3. Serve right away. Enjoy!

Herbed Roasted Potatoes

Servings: 4
Total Time: 24 Minutes
Calories: 208
Fat: 7.1 g
Protein: 3.6 g
Carbs: 33.8 g
Fiber: 3 g

Ingredients and Quantity
- 1 tsp. crushed, dried thyme
- 1 tsp. ground black pepper
- 2 tbsp. olive oil
- 1/2 tbsp. crushed, dried rosemary
- 3 potatoes, peeled, washed and cut into wedges
- 1/2 tsp. seasoned salt

Direction
1. Lay the potatoes in the air fryer cooking basket, drizzle olive oil over your potatoes.
2. Then, cook for 17 minutes at 353 degrees F.
3. Toss with the seasonings and serve warm with your favorite salad on the side. Enjoy!

Indian-Style Garnet Sweet Potatoes

Servings: 4
Total Time: 24 Minutes
Calories: 103
Fat: 9.1 g
Protein: 1.9 g
Carbs: 4.9 g
Fiber: 1.2 g

Ingredients and Quantity
- 1/3 tsp. white pepper
- 1 tbsp. butter, melted
- 1/2 tsp. turmeric powder
- 5 garnet sweet potatoes, peeled and diced
- 1 1/2 tbsp. maple syrup
- 2 tsp. tamarind paste
- 1 1/2 tbsp. fresh lime juice
- 1 1/2 tsp. ground allspice

Direction
1. In a mixing bowl, toss all ingredients until sweet potatoes are well coated.
2. Air-fry them at 335 degrees F for 12 minutes.
3. Pause the air fryer and toss again.
4. Increase the temperature to 390 degrees F and cook for an additional 10 minutes.
5. Eat warm. Enjoy!

Easy Frizzled Leeks

Servings: 6
Total Time: 52 Minutes
Calories: 291
Fat: 6 g
Protein: 5.7 g
Carbs: 53.3 g
Fiber: 4.3 g

Ingredients and Quantity
- 1/2 tsp. porcini powder
- 1 1/2 cup rice flour
- 1 tbsp. vegetable oil
- 3 medium-sized leeks, sliced into julienne strips
- 2 large-sized dishes with ice water
- 2 tsp. onion powder
- Fine sea salt and cayenne pepper, to taste

Direction
1. Allow the leeks to soak in ice water for about 25 minutes; drain well.
2. Place the rice flour, salt, cayenne pepper, onions powder, and porcini powder into a resealable bag.
3. Add the celery and shake to coat well.
4. Drizzle vegetable oil over the seasoned leeks.
5. Air fry at 390 degrees F for about 18 minutes; turn them halfway through the cooking time.
6. Serve with homemade mayonnaise or any other sauce for dipping. Enjoy!

Easy Sautéed Green Beans

Servings: 4
Total Time: 12 Minutes
Calories: 53
Fat: 3 g
Protein: 1.6 g
Carbs: 6.1 g
Fiber: 1.2 g

Ingredients and Quantity
- 3/4 pound green beans, cleaned
- 1 tbsp. balsamic vinegar
- 1/4 tsp. kosher salt
- 1/2 tsp. mixed peppercorns, freshly cracked
- 1 tbsp. butter
- Sesame seeds, to serve

Direction
1. Set your air fryer to cook at 390 F.
2. Mix the green beans with all of the above ingredients, apart from the sesame seeds.
3. Set the timer for 10 minutes.
4. Meanwhile, toast the sesame seeds in a small-sized nonstick skillet; make sure to stir continuously.
5. Serve sautéed green beans on a nice serving platter sprinkled with toasted sesame seeds. Enjoy!

Ricotta and Scallion Stuffed Potatoes

Servings: 4
Total Time: 15 Minutes
Calories: 290
Fat: 14.4 g
Protein: 1.4 g
Carbs: 32.5 g
Fiber: 1.4 g

Ingredients and Quantity
- 4 baking potatoes
- 2 tbsp. olive oil
- 1/2 cup Ricotta cheese, room temperature
- 2 tbsp. scallions, chopped
- 1 heaping tbsp. fresh parsley, roughly chopped
- 1 heaping tbsp. coriander, minced
- 2 oz. cheddar cheese, preferably freshly grated
- 1 tsp. celery seeds
- 1/2 tsp. salt
- 1/2 tsp. garlic pepper

Direction
1. Firstly, prick your potatoes with a small paring knife.
2. Cook them in the Air Fryer cooking basket for approximately 13 minutes at 350 degrees F. Check for doneness and cook for 2-3 minutes longer if needed.
3. Meanwhile, make the stuffing by mixing the other items.
4. When your potatoes are thoroughly cooked, open them up.
5. Divide the stuffing among all potatoes and serve on individual plates. Enjoy!

Easy Cheesy Cauliflower and Broccoli

Servings: 6
Total Time: 20 Minutes
Calories: 133
Fat: 9.5 g
Protein: 5.9 g
Carbs: 9.5 g
Fiber: 3.2 g

Ingredients and Quantity
- 1 pound cauliflower florets
- 1 pound broccoli florets
- 2 1/2 tbsp. sesame oil
- 1/2 tsp. smoked cayenne pepper
- 3/4 tsp. sea salt flakes
- 1 tbsp. lemon zest, grated
- 1/2 cup Colby cheese, shredded

Direction
1. Prepare the cauliflower and broccoli using your favorite steaming method.
2. Then, drain them well; add the sesame oil, cayenne pepper, and salt flakes.
3. Air-fry at 390 degrees F for approximately 16 minutes; make sure to check the vegetables halfway through the cooking time.
4. Afterwards, stir in the lemon zest and Colby cheese.
5. Toss to coat well and serve immediately!

Peppery Vegetable Omelet with Cheese

Servings: 2
Total Time: 15 Minutes
Calories: 317
Fat: 19.8 g
Protein: 10.2 g
Carbs: 16.5 g
Fiber: 2 g

Ingredients and Quantity
- 3 tbsp. plain milk
- 4 eggs, whisked
- 1 tsp. melted butter
- Kosher salt and freshly ground black pepper, to taste
- 1 red bell pepper, deveined and chopped
- 1 green bell pepper, deveined and chopped
- 1 white onion, freshly chopped
- 1/2 cup baby spinach leaves, roughly chopped
- 1/2 cup Halloumi cheese, shaved

Direction
1. Start with spreading the canola cooking spray onto the Air Fryer baking pan.
2. Add all of the above ingredients to the baking pan; give them a good stir.
3. Then, set your machine to cook at 350 degrees F; cook your omelet for 13 minutes.
4. Serve warm and enjoy!

Mushrooms and Peppers in Puff Pastry

Servings: 4
Total Time: 25 Minutes
Calories: 533
Fat: 38.7 g
Protein: 8.4 g
Carbs: 39.1 g
Fiber: 2.5 g

Ingredients and Quantity

- 1 1/2 tbsp. sesame oil
- 1 cup sliced white mushrooms
- 2 garlic cloves, minced
- 1 bell pepper, seeded and chopped
- 1/4 tsp. sea salt
- 1/4 tsp. dried rosemary
- 1/2 tsp. ground black pepper, or more to taste
- 11 oz. puff pastry sheets
- 1/2 cup crème fraiche
- 1 egg, well whisked
- 1/2 cup parmesan cheese, preferably freshly grated

Direction

1. Start by preheating your Air Fryer to 400 degrees F.
2. Then, heat the sesame oil in a skillet that is placed over a moderate heat; cook the mushrooms, garlic, and pepper until tender and fragrant.
3. Season with salt, rosemary, and pepper.
4. Meanwhile, roll out the puff pastry; cut into 4-inch squares.
5. Evenly spread the crème fraiche on them.
6. Then, divide the vegetables among the puff pastry squares.
7. Fold each square diagonally over the filling in order to form a triangle shape.
8. Pinch the edges and coat each triangle with whisked egg.
9. Coat them with grated Parmesan.
10. Cook for 22 to 25 minutes. Serve and enjoy!

Celery and Carrot Croquettes with Chive Mayo

Servings: 4
Total Time: 10 Minutes
Calories: 124
Fat: 2 g
Protein: 4.8 g
Carbs: 21.9 g
Fiber: 3 g

Ingredients and Quantity

- 2 medium-sized carrots, trimmed and grated
- 2 medium-sized celery stalks, trimmed and grated
- 1/2 cup leek, finely chopped
- 1 tbsp. garlic paste
- 1/4 tsp. freshly cracked black pepper
- 1 tsp. fine sea salt
- 1 tbsp. fresh dill, finely chopped
- 1 egg, lightly whisked
- 1/4 cup all-purpose flour
- 1/4 tsp. baking powder
- 1/2 cup breadcrumbs (seasoned or regular)
- Chive mayo, to serve

Direction

1. Place the carrots and celery on a paper towel and squeeze them to remove excess liquid.
2. Combine the vegetables with the other ingredients, except the breadcrumbs and chive mayo.
3. Shape the balls using 1 tablespoon of the vegetable mixture.
4. Then, gently flatten each ball with your palm or a wide spatula.
5. Coat them with breadcrumbs, covering all sides.
6. Spritz the croquettes with a non - stick cooking oil.
7. Air-fry the vegetable croquettes in a single layer for 6 minutes at 360 degrees F.
8. Serve warm with chive mayo. Enjoy!

Scrambled Eggs with Spinach and Tomato

Servings: 2
Total Time: 15 Minutes
Calories: 274
Fat: 23.2 g
Protein: 13.7 g
Carbs: 5.7 g
Fiber: 2.6 g

Ingredients and Quantity

- 2 tbsp. olive oil, melted
- 4 eggs, whisked
- 5 oz. fresh spinach, chopped
- 1 medium sized tomato, chopped
- 1 tsp. fresh lemon juice
- 1/2 tsp. coarse salt
- 1/2 tsp. ground black pepper
- 1/2 cup fresh basil, roughly chopped

Direction

1. Add the olive oil to an Air Fryer baking pan.
2. Make sure to tilt the pan to spread the oil evenly.
3. Simply combine the remaining ingredients, except for the basil leaves; whisk well until everything is well incorporated.
4. Cook in the preheated Air Fryer for 8 to 12 minutes at 280 degrees F.
5. Garnish with fresh basil leaves.
6. Serve warm with a dollop of sour cream if desired. Enjoy!

Colby Potato Patties

Servings: 8
Total Time: 15 Minutes
Calories: 291
Fat: 18 g
Protein: 9.3 g
Carbs: 23.7 g
Fiber: 1.7 g

Ingredients and Quantity

- 2 pounds white potatoes, peeled and grated
- 1/2 cup scallions, finely chopped
- 1/2 tsp. freshly ground black pepper, or more, to taste
- 1 tbsp. fine sea salt
- 1/2 tsp. hot paprika
- 2 cups Colby cheese, shredded
- 1/4 cup canola oil
- 1 cup crushed crackers

Direction

1. Firstly, boil the potatoes until fork tender.
2. Drain, peel and mash your potatoes.
3. Thoroughly mix the mashed potatoes with scallions, pepper, salt, paprika, and cheese.
4. Then, shape the balls using your hands.
5. Now, flatten the balls to make the patties.
6. In a shallow bowl, mix canola oil with crushed crackers.
7. Roll the patties over the crumb mixture.
8. Next, cook your patties at 360 degrees F approximately 10 minutes, working in batches.
9. Serve with tabasco mayo if desired. Enjoy!

Hash Brown Casserole

Servings: 6
Total Time: 23 Minutes
Calories: 195
Fat: 11.1 g
Protein: 3.1 g
Carbs: 22 g
Fiber: 3 g

Ingredients and Quantity

- 1/2 cup cheddar cheese, shredded
- 1 tbsp. soft cheese, at room temperature
- 1/3 cup crushed bran cereal
- 1 1/2 yellow or white medium-sized onion, chopped
- 5 oz. condensed cream of celery soup
- 1 tbsp. fresh cilantro, finely minced
- 1/3 cup sour cream
- 3 garlic cloves, peeled and finely minced
- 2 cups hash brown potatoes, shredded
- 1 1/2 tbsp. margarine or butter, melted
- Sea salt and freshly ground black pepper, to taste
- Crushed red pepper flakes, to taste

Direction

1. Grab a large-sized bowl and whisk the celery soup, sour cream, soft cheese, red pepper, salt, and black pepper.
2. Stir in the hash browns, onion, garlic, cilantro, and Cheddar cheese.
3. Mix until everything is thoroughly combined.
4. Scrape the mixture into a baking dish that is previously lightly greased.
5. In another mixing bowl, combine together the bran cereal and melted margarine (or butter).
6. Spread the mixture evenly over the top of the hash brown mixture.
7. Bake for 17 minutes at 290 degrees F.
8. Eat warm, garnished with some extra sour cream if desired. Enjoy!

Pepper Jack Cauliflower Bites

Servings: 2
Total Time: 24 Minutes
Calories: 271
Fat: 23 g
Protein: 9.8 g
Carbs: 8.9 g
Fiber: 2.8 g

Ingredients and Quantity

- 1/3 tsp. shallot powder
- 1 tsp. ground black pepper
- 1 1/2 large-sized heads of cauliflower, broken into florets
- 1/4 tsp. cumin powder
- 1/2 tsp. garlic salt
- 1/4 cup pepper Jack cheese, grated
- 1 1/2 tbsp. vegetable oil
- 1/3 tsp. paprika

Direction

1. Boil cauliflower in a large pan of salted water approximately 5 minutes.
2. After that, drain the cauliflower florets; now, transfer them to a baking dish.
3. Toss the cauliflower florets with the rest of the above ingredients.
4. Roast at 395 degrees F for 16 minutes, turn them halfway through the process. Enjoy!

Cheesy Broccoli Croquettes

Servings: 6
Total Time: 50 Minutes
Calories: 246
Fat: 14 g
Protein: 14.5 g
Carbs: 15.2 g
Fiber: 1.6 g

Ingredients and Quantity
- 1 1/2 cups Monterey Jack cheese
- 1 tsp. dried dill weed
- 1/3 tsp. ground black pepper
- 3 eggs, whisked
- 1 tsp. cayenne pepper
- 1/2 tsp. kosher salt
- 1 cup Panko crumbs
- 2 1/2 cups broccoli florets
- 1/3 cup parmesan cheese

Direction
1. Blitz the broccoli florets in a food processor until finely crumbed.
2. Then, combine the broccoli with the rest of the above ingredients.
3. Roll the mixture into small balls; place the balls in the fridge for approximately half an hour.
4. Preheat your air fryer to 335 degrees F and set the timer to 14 minutes; cook until broccoli croquettes are browned and serve warm. Enjoy!

Cauliflower Cakes Ole

Servings: 6
Total Time: 48 Minutes
Calories: 190
Fat: 14.1 g
Protein: 11.5 g
Carbs: 4.7 g
Fiber: 1.3 g

Ingredients and Quantity
- 2 tsp. chili powder
- 1 1/2 tsp. kosher salt
- 1 tsp. dried marjoram, crushed
- 2 1/2 cups cauliflower, broken into florets
- 1 1/3 cups tortilla chip crumbs
- 1/2 tsp. crushed red pepper flakes
- 3 eggs, whisked
- 1 1/2 cups Queso cotija cheese, crumbled

Direction
1. Blitz the cauliflower florets in your food processor until they're crumbled (it is the size of rice).
2. Then, combine the cauliflower "rice" with the other items.
3. Now, roll the cauliflower mixture into small balls; refrigerate for 30 minutes.
4. Preheat your air fryer to 345 degrees and set the timer for 14 minutes; cook until the balls are browned and serve right away. Enjoy!

Celery and Carrot Croquettes

Servings: 4
Total Time: 25 Minutes
Calories: 142
Fat: 6 g
Protein: 7.2 g
Carbs: 15.8 g
Fiber: 3 g

Ingredients and Quantity
- 2 small eggs, lightly beaten
- 1/3 tsp. freshly cracked black pepper
- 1/3 cup Colby cheese, grated
- 1/2 tbsp. fresh dill, finely chopped
- 1/2 tbsp. garlic paste
- 1/3 cup onion, finely chopped
- 1/3 cup all-purpose flour
- 3 medium-sized carrots, trimmed and grated
- 2 tsp. fine sea salt
- 3 medium-sized celery stalks, trimmed and grated
- 1/3 tsp. baking powder

Direction
1. Place the carrots and celery on a paper towel and squeeze them to remove the excess liquid.
2. Combine the vegetables with the other ingredients in the order listed above.
3. Shape the balls using 1 tablespoon of the vegetable mixture.
4. Then, gently flatten each ball with your palm or a wide spatula.
5. Spritz the croquettes with a nonstick cooking oil.
6. Bake the vegetable cakes in a single layer for 17 minutes at 318 degrees F.
7. Serve warm with sour cream. Enjoy!

Smoked Veggie Omelet

Servings: 2
Total Time: 14 Minutes
Calories: 226
Fat: 11.5 g
Protein: 16.3 g
Carbs: 14.2 g
Fiber: 5 g

Ingredients and Quantity
- 1/3 cup cherry tomatoes, chopped
- 1 bell pepper, seeded and chopped
- 1/3 tsp. freshly ground black pepper
- 1/2 purple onion, peeled and sliced
- 1 tsp. smoked cayenne pepper
- 5 medium-sized eggs, well beaten
- 1/3 cup smoked tofu, crumbled
- 1 tsp. seasoned salt
- 1 1/2 tbsp. fresh chives, chopped

Direction
1. Brush a baking dish with a spray coating.
2. Throw all ingredients, minus fresh chives, into the baking dish; give it a good stir.
3. Cook about 15 minutes at 325 degrees F.
4. Garnish with fresh chopped chives. Serve and enjoy!

Sweet Potato and Carrot Croquettes

Servings: 4
Total Time: 22 Minutes
Calories: 206
Fat: 5 g
Protein: 8.3 g
Carbs: 32 g
Fiber: 2.1 g

Ingredients and Quantity

- 1/3 cup Swiss cheese, grated
- 1/3 tsp. fine sea salt
- 1/3 tsp. baking powder
- 1/3 cup scallions, finely chopped
- 3 carrots, trimmed and grated
- 1/2 tsp. freshly cracked black pepper
- 3 sweet potatoes, grated
- 1/3 cup all-purpose flour
- 2 small eggs, lightly beaten

Direction

1. Place grated sweet potatoes and carrots on a paper towel and pat them dry.
2. Combine the potatoes and carrots with the other ingredients in the order listed above.
3. Then, create the balls using 1½ tablespoons of the vegetable mixture.
4. Then, gently flatten each ball.
5. Spritz the croquettes with a nonstick cooking oil.
6. Bake your croquettes for 13 minutes at 305 degrees F; work with batches.
7. Serve warm with tomato ketchup and mayonnaise. Enjoy!

Manchego and Potato Patties

Servings: 8
Total Time: 15 Minutes
Calories: 191
Fat: 8.7 g
Protein: 7 g
Carbs: 22 g
Fiber: 1.4 g

Ingredients and Quantity

- 1 cup Manchego cheese, shredded
- 1 tsp. paprika
- 1 tsp. freshly ground black pepper
- 1/2 tbsp. fine sea salt
- 2 cups scallions, finely chopped
- 2 pounds Russet potatoes, peeled and grated
- 2 tbsp. canola oil
- 2 tsp. dried basil

Direction

1. Thoroughly combine all of the above ingredients.
2. Then, shape the balls using your hands.
3. Now, flatten the balls to make the patties.
4. Next, cook your patties at 360 degrees F approximately 10 minutes. Serve and enjoy!

Mint-Butter Stuffed Mushrooms

Servings: 3
Total Time: 20 Minutes
Calories: 290
Fat: 14.7 g
Protein: 28 g
Carbs: 13.4 g
Fiber: 3.3 g

Ingredients and Quantity
- 3 garlic cloves, minced
- 1 tsp. ground black pepper, or more, to taste
- 1/3 cup seasoned breadcrumbs
- 1 1/2 tbsp. fresh mint, chopped
- 1 tsp. salt, or more, to taste
- 1 1/2 tbsp. melted butter
- 14 medium-sized mushrooms, cleaned, stalks removed

Direction
1. Mix all of the above ingredients, minus the mushrooms, in a mixing bowl to prepare the filling.
2. Then, stuff the mushrooms with the prepared filling.
3. Air-fry stuffed mushrooms at 375 degrees F for about 12 minutes.
4. Taste for doneness and serve at room temperature as a vegetarian appetizer. Enjoy!

Ricotta and Leafy Green Omelet

Servings: 2
Total Time: 17 Minutes
Calories: 409
Fat: 29.5 g
Protein: 27.9 g
Carbs: 6.9 g
Fiber: 3 g

Ingredients and Quantity
- 1/3 cup Ricotta cheese
- 5 eggs, beaten
- 1/2 red bell pepper, seeded and sliced
- 1 cup mixed greens, roughly chopped
- 1/2 green bell pepper, seeded and sliced
- 1/2 tsp. dried basil
- 1/2 chipotle pepper, finely minced
- 1/2 tsp. dried oregano

Direction
1. Lightly coat the inside of a baking dish with a pan spray.
2. Then, throw all ingredients into the baking dish; give it a good stir.
3. Bake at 325 degrees F for 15 minutes. Serve and enjoy!

Zesty Broccoli with Hot Sauce

Servings: 6
Total Time: 20 Minutes
Calories: 80
Fat: 3.8 g
Protein: 2.5 g
Carbs: 10.8 g
Fiber: 4.5 g

Ingredients and Quantity

For the Broccoli Bites:

- 1 medium-sized head broccoli, broken into florets
- 1/2 tsp. lemon zest, freshly grated
- 1/3 tsp. fine sea salt
- 1/2 tsp. hot paprika
- 1 tsp. shallot powder
- 1 tsp. porcini powder
- 1/2 tsp. granulated garlic
- 1/3 tsp. celery seeds
- 1 1/2 tbsp. olive oil

For the Hot Sauce:

- 1/2 cup tomato sauce
- 3 tbsp. brown sugar
- 1 tbsp. balsamic vinegar
- 1/2 tsp. ground allspice

Direction

1. Toss all the ingredients for the broccoli bites in a mixing bowl, covering the broccoli florets on all sides.
2. Cook them in the preheated Air Fryer at 360 degrees for 13 to 15 minutes.
3. In the meantime, mix all ingredients for the hot sauce.
4. Pause your Air Fryer, mix the broccoli with the prepared sauce and cook for further 3 minutes. Serve and enjoy!

Sweet Corn and Kernel Fritters

Servings: 4
Total Time: 20 Minutes
Calories: 275
Fat: 8.4 g
Protein: 15.7 g
Carbs: 40.5 g
Fiber: 6 g

Ingredients and Quantity
- 1 medium sized carrot, grated
- 1 yellow onion, finely chopped
- 4 oz. canned sweet corn kernels, drained
- 1 tsp. sea salt flakes
- 1 heaping tbsp., fresh cilantro, chopped
- 1 medium-sized egg, whisked
- 2 tbsp. plain milk
- 1 cup parmesan cheese, grated
- 1/4 cup self-rising flour
- 1/3 tsp. baking powder
- 1/3 brown sugar

Direction
1. Press down the grated carrot in the colander to remove excess liquid.
2. Then, spread the grated carrot between several sheets of kitchen towels and pat it dry.
3. Then, mix the carrots with the remaining ingredients in the order listed above.
4. Roll 1 tablespoon of the mixture into a ball; gently flatten it using the back of a spoon or your hand.
5. Now, repeat with the remaining ingredients.
6. Spitz the balls with a nonstick cooking oil.
7. Cook in a single layer at 350 degrees for 8 to 11 minutes or until they're firm to touch in the center.
8. Serve warm and enjoy!

Gorgonzola Stuffed Mushrooms with Horseradish Mayo

Servings: 5
Total Time: 15 Minutes
Calories: 210
Fat: 15.2 g
Protein: 7.6 g
Carbs: 13.6 g
Fiber: 2.7 g

Ingredients and Quantity
- 1/2 cup breadcrumbs
- 2 garlic cloves, pressed
- 2 tbsp. fresh coriander, chopped
- 1/3 tsp. kosher salt
- 1/2 tsp. crushed red pepper flakes
- 1 1/2 tbsp. olive oil
- 20 medium-sized mushrooms, cut off the stems
- 1/2 cup Gorgonzola cheese, grated
- 1/4 cup low fat mayonnaise
- 1 tsp. prepared horseradish, well drained
- 1 tbsp. fresh parsley, finely chopped

Direction
1. Mix the breadcrumbs together with the garlic, coriander, salt, red pepper, and the olive oil; mix to combine well.
2. Stuff the mushroom caps with the breadcrumb filling.
3. Top with grated Gorgonzola.
4. Place the mushrooms in the Air Fryer grill pan and slide them into the machine.
5. Grill them at 380 degrees F for 8 to 12 minutes or until the stuffing is warmed through.
6. Meanwhile, prepare the horseradish mayo by mixing the mayonnaise, horseradish and parsley.
7. Serve with the warm fried mushrooms. Enjoy!

Basic Pepper French Fries

Servings: 4
Total Time: 33 Minutes
Calories: 263
Fat: 9.1 g
Protein: 4.5 g
Carbs: 42 g
Fiber: 3 g

Ingredients and Quantity
- 1 tsp. fine sea salt
- 1/2 tsp. freshly ground black pepper
- 2 1/2 tbsp. canola oil
- 6 Russet potatoes, cut them into fries
- 1/2 tsp. crushed red pepper flakes

Direction
1. Start by preheating your air fryer to 340 degrees F.
2. Place the fries in your air fryer and toss them with the oil.
3. Add the seasonings and toss again.
4. Cook for 30 minutes, shaking your fries several times.
5. Taste for doneness and eat warm. Enjoy!

Oyster Mushroom and Lemongrass Omelet

Servings: 2
Total Time: 42 Minutes
Calories: 362
Fat: 29 g
Protein: 19 g
Carbs: 7.2 g
Fiber: 2.8 g

Ingredients and Quantity
- 3 king oyster mushrooms, thinly sliced
- 1 lemongrass, chopped
- 1/2 tsp. dried marjoram
- 5 eggs
- 1/3 cup Swiss cheese, grated
- 2 tbsp. sour cream
- 1 1/2 tsp. dried rosemary
- 2 tsp. red pepper flakes, crushed
- 2 tbsp. butter, melted
- 1/2 red onion, peeled and sliced into thin rounds
- 1/2 tsp. garlic powder
- 1 tsp. dried dill weed
- Fine sea salt and ground black pepper, to taste

Direction
1. Melt the margarine in a skillet that is placed over a medium flame.
2. Then, sweat the onion, mushrooms and lemongrass until they softened; reserve.
3. Then, preheat the air fryer to 325 F.
4. Then, crack the eggs into a mixing bowl and whisk them well.
5. Then, fold in the sour cream and give it a good stir.
6. Now, stir in the salt, black pepper, red pepper, rosemary, garlic powder, marjoram, and dill.
7. Next step, grease the inside of an air fryer baking dish with a thin layer of a cooking spray.
8. Pour the egg/seasoning mixture into the baking dish; throw in the reserved mixture.
9. Top with the Swiss cheese.
10. Set the timer for 35 minutes; cook until a knife inserted in the center comes out clean and dry. Serve and enjoy!

Spinach and Cheese Stuffed Baked Potatoes

Servings: 4
Total Time: 18 Minutes
Calories: 327
Fat: 7 g
Protein: 9.4 g
Carbs: 59 g
Fiber: 2.2 g

Ingredients and Quantity
- 3 tbsp. extra-virgin olive oil
- 2/3 cup sour cream, at room temperature
- 1 1/2 cup baby spinach leaves, torn into small pieces
- 3 pounds Russet potatoes
- 2 garlic cloves, peeled and finely minced
- 1/4 tsp. fine sea salt, or more, to taste
- 1/3 cup cheddar cheese, freshly grated

Direction
1. Firstly, stab the potatoes with a fork.
2. Preheat the air fryer to 345 degrees F.
3. Now, cook the potatoes for 14 minutes.
4. Meanwhile, make the filling by mixing the rest of the above items.
5. Afterward that, open the potatoes up and stuff them with the prepared filling. Serve and enjoy!

Pantano Romanesco with Goat Cheese Appetizer

Servings: 4
Total Time: 20 Minutes
Calories: 237
Fat: 20.4 g
Protein: 13 g
Carbs: 0.9 g
Fiber: 0.9 g

Ingredients and Quantity
- 6 oz. goat cheese, sliced
- 2 shallots, thinly sliced
- 2 Pantano Romanesco tomatoes, cut into 1/2 inch slices
- 1 1/2 tbsp. extra virgin olive oil
- 3/4 tsp. sea salt
- Fresh parsley, for garnish
- Fresh basil, chopped

Direction
1. Preheat your air fryer to 380 degrees F.
2. Now, pat each tomato slice dry using a paper towel.
3. Sprinkle each slice with salt and chopped basil.
4. Top with a slice of goat cheese.
5. Top with the shallot slices; drizzle with olive oil.
6. Add the prepared tomato and feta "bites" to the air fryer food basket.
7. Cook in the air fryer for about 14 minutes.
8. Lastly, adjust seasonings to taste and serve garnished with fresh parsley leaves. Enjoy!

Swiss Chard and Cheese Omelet

Servings: 2
Total Time: 25 Minutes
Calories: 388
Fat: 27 g
Protein: 29 g
Carbs: 6 g
Fiber: 2.6 g

Ingredients and Quantity

- 1 tsp. garlic paste
- 1 1/2 tsp. olive oil
- 1/2 cup crème fraiche
- 1/3 tsp. ground black pepper, to taste
- 1/3 cup Swiss cheese, crumbled
- 1 tsp. cayenne pepper
- 1/3 cup Swiss chard, torn into pieces
- 5 eggs
- 1/4 cup yellow onions, chopped
- 1 tsp. fine sea salt

Direction

1. Crack your eggs into a mixing dish; then, add the crème fraîche, salt, ground black pepper, and cayenne pepper.
2. Next, coat the inside of a baking dish with olive oil and tilt it to spread evenly.
3. Scrape the egg/cream mixture into the baking dish.
4. Add the other ingredients; mix to combine well.
5. Bake for 18 minutes at 292 degrees F. Serve immediately. Enjoy!

Mom's Jack Potatoes

Servings: 4
Total Time: 23 Minutes
Calories: 270
Fat: 10.9 g
Protein: 8.8 g
Carbs: 35.2 g
Fiber: 2.8 g

Ingredients and Quantity

- 1/3 cottage cheese, softened
- 1/3 cup Parmigiano-Reggiano cheese, grated
- 1 tsp. black pepper
- 1 1/2 heaping tbsp. roughly chopped cilantro leaves
- 1/3 cup green onions, freshly chopped
- 5 average-sized potatoes
- 2 1/2 tbsp. softened butter
- 1 tsp. salt

Direction

1. Firstly, stab your potatoes with a fork.
2. Cook them in the air fryer basket for 20 minutes at 345 degrees F.
3. While the potatoes are cooking, make the filling by mixing the rest of the above ingredients.
4. Afterward, open the potatoes up and stuff them with the prepared filling. Serve and enjoy!

Skinny Asparagus and Mushroom Casserole

Servings: 2
Total Time: 27 Minutes
Calories: 207
Fat: 19.7 g
Protein: 20.6 g
Carbs: 30.2 g
Fiber: 3.7 g

Ingredients and Quantity
- 1/3 cup milk
- 1/3 cup Colby cheese, grated
- 5 slices Italian bread, cut into cubes
- 1 1/2 cups white mushrooms, sliced
- 2 asparagus spears, chopped
- 1 tsp. table salt, or to taste
- 2 well-beaten eggs
- 1/3 tsp. smoked cayenne pepper
- 1 tsp. ground black pepper, or to taste
- 1/3 tsp. dried rosemary, crushed

Direction
1. Throw the bread cubes into the baking dish.
2. In a mixing dish, thoroughly combine the eggs and milk.
3. Stir in 1/2 of cheese; add the seasonings.
4. Pour 3/4 of egg/cheese mixture over the bread cubes in the baking dish; press gently using a wide spatula.
5. Now, top with the mushrooms and chopped asparagus.
6. Pour the remaining egg/cheese mixture over the top; make sure to spread it evenly.
7. Top with the remaining Colby cheese and bake for 20 minutes at 325 degrees F. Serve and enjoy!

Winter Sausage with Root Vegetables

Servings: 4
Total Time: 30 Minutes
Calories: 289
Fat: 13.6 g
Protein: 13.3 g
Carbs: 32.5 g
Fiber: 6.7 g

Ingredients and Quantity
- 1/2 pound Italian sausage
- 3 sprigs rosemary
- 1 medium-sized parsnip, sliced
- 1/3 pound fingerling potatoes
- 3 sprigs thyme
- 1/3 pounds carrots, trimmed and cut into matchsticks
- 1/2 celery stalk, sliced
- 2 garlic cloves, smashed
- 2 tbsp. extra-virgin olive oil
- 3 small-sized leeks, cut into halves lengthwise
- A pinch grated nutmeg
- Salt and black pepper, to taste

Direction
1. Arrange fingerling potatoes, carrots, celery, parsnip, and leeks on the bottom of the air fryer baking dish.
2. Tuck the garlic cloves around the vegetables.
3. Sprinkle with the seasonings and top with the sausage.
4. Roast approximately 33 minutes at 375 degrees F, stirring occasionally. Serve and enjoy!

SECTION 2: VEGAN AND VEGETARIAN AIR FRYER LOW FAT RECIPES
Breakfast Recipes

Toasted Coconut French Toast

Servings: 1
Total Time: 9 Minutes
Ingredients and Quantity

- 2 slices gluten-free bread
- 1/2 cup unsweetened shredded coconut
- 1/2 cup unsweetened coconut milk
- 1 tsp. baking powder

Direction

1. In a wide rimmed shallow bowl, mix the coconut milk and baking powder and set aside.
2. In another shallow bowl, spread the shredded coconut out into an even layer.
3. Take each slice of the gluten-free bread and soak it in the coconut milk mixture for a few seconds.
4. Transfer the soaked slice to the shredded coconut bowl and fully coat the slice in the shredded coconut.
5. Carefully place both slices of the coconut bread in your air fryer and close.
6. Cook at 350 degrees Fahrenheit for 4 minutes.
7. Once done, remove and top with honey, maple syrup or your favorite topping. Enjoy!

Vegan Breakfast Ranchero

Servings: 2
Total Time: 13 Minutes
Ingredients and Quantity

- 2 large flour gluten-free tortillas
- 2 small corn tortillas
- 2 servings vegan scramble or tofu scramble
- 1/2 to 1 cup classic jarred Ranchero sauce
- 1/2 to 3/4 avocado, peeled and sliced lengthways
- 1 to 2 fresh jalapenos, stemmed, pitted and sliced
- 1/3 cup cooked pinto beans

Direction

1. Arrange the large flour tortillas onto your work surface.
2. Assemble the wraps by stacking all ingredients in to the tortilla in this order - egg or tofu scramble, the jalapeno, jarred Ranchero sauce, fresh corn tortillas, sliced avocado and finally the cooked pinto beans.
3. You may add additional ranchero sauce as per your preference.
4. Fold the flour tortilla around the fillings until they are completely sealed. It should resemble a traditional burrito.
5. Cook in the air fryer at 350 degrees Fahrenheit for 6 minutes and then bake in the oven at 325 degrees Fahrenheit for 5-8 minutes, until warm and slightly crispy.
6. Finally, pan fry in dry pan at a medium-low heat for a 2 - 3 minutes on each side, until crisp and golden brown.
7. Serve immediately with traditional Mexican toppings like sour cream, guacamole or Queso fresco.

Pecan French Toast

Servings: 12
Total Time: 20 Minutes
Ingredients and Quantity

- 8 pieces whole-grain, gluten-free, vegan bread
- 1 cup rolled oats
- 1 cup pecans, (or any other nut of your choice)
- 2 tbsp. ground flax seed
- 3/4 cup almond milk (plain or vanilla-flavored)
- 1 tsp. ground cinnamon

For Serving:

- Real maple syrup

Direction

1. Make the topping for the toast by mixing the flaxseeds, oats, pecans and ground cinnamon to a food processor and pulse until the mixture resembles coarse bread crumbs.
2. Pour into a shallow bowl that's large enough to dip in the bread slices.
3. Add the almond milk to a medium-sized bowl and then briefly soak one or two pieces of the bread for 15 seconds, then flip over and soak the other side. Be careful that the bread does not become mushy.
4. Place the amount of slices that fit into the air fryer basket in a single layer and cook at 350 degrees Fahrenheit for 3 minutes, then flip the bread over and cook for a further 3 minutes.
5. Repeat until all the bread slices are done.
6. Top with maple syrup or any other toppings of your choice and enjoy!

German Pancakes

Servings: 5
Total Time: 13 Minutes
Ingredients and Quantity

- 1 cup whole wheat flour or oat flour
- 1 cup almond milk
- 2 heaping tbsp. all-natural applesauce
- 3 flax eggs
- 1/8 tsp. sea salt

For Garnishing (Optional):

- French berries
- Icing sugar
- Raw unsweetened cocoa nibs
- Plain Greek yogurt
- Real honey or maple syrup

Direction

1. Preheat the air fryer to 390 degrees Fahrenheit.
2. Set a cast-iron tray or ceramic oven-proof ramekin inside the air fryer so that it heats as the air fryer heats up.
3. Add all the ingredients for the pancake batter to a blender and blend the mixture until smooth. You may thin out the mixture with almond milk or applesauce, if it seems too thick.
4. Spray the cast iron tray or ceramic ramekin with cooking oil spray, and then pour in the pancake batter, one serving at a time.
5. Air fry the pancakes for 6 - 8 minutes. The top of the pancake may come out slightly hard, but this is okay as no oil has been used to cook them and the pancakes will soften as they cool.
6. Garnish with the topping of your choice and enjoy!
7. **Note:** This batter can be stored in an airtight container in the fridge for 2 to 3 days.

Sweet Potato Toast

Servings: 2
Total Time: 35 Minutes
Ingredients and Quantity
- 1 sweet potato
- 1 tbsp. seasoning
- Cooking oil spray

Direction
1. Preheat the air fryer to 375 degrees Fahrenheit.
2. Trim both ends of the sweet potato.
3. Slice lengthwise into ⅓-inch thick slices.
4. Coat the sweet potato with cooking oil spray and season.
5. When the air fryer is hot, remove the basket and layer the sweet potato slices.
6. Air fry for 15 minutes, and then flip over and air fry for a further 15 minutes.
7. Top with your topping of choice and enjoy!

Oatmeal with Raspberries

Servings: 2
Total Time: 20 Minutes
Ingredients and Quantity
- 3 oz. oatmeal
- 2 ripe bananas, peeled and mashed
- 1 cup almond milk
- 4 oz. frozen raspberries
- 1/8 tsp. salt

Direction
1. Preheat the air fryer at 350 degrees Fahrenheit or an oven to 400 degrees Fahrenheit.
2. Using a fork, mash the bananas in a ceramic oven-proof dish and then add then oatmeal, milk and salt.
3. Stir well to mix and then add the frozen raspberries mixing through well.
4. Cook in the air fryer or oven for 15 minutes.
5. Slice and serve immediately, topped with yoghurt and honey!

Easy Tofu Scramble

Servings: 3
Total Time: 35 Minutes
Ingredients and Quantity
- 2 1/2 cups (2 to 3) red potatoes, chopped into 1 inch cubes
- 4 cups broccoli florets
- 1/2 cup chopped onion
- 2 tbsp. light soy sauce
- 2 tbsp. olive oil, divided into 2portions
- 1 tsp. ground turmeric
- 1/2 tsp. onion powder
- 1/2 tsp. garlic powder

Direction
1. In a medium-sized bowl, mix the tofu, olive oil, soy sauce, garlic powder, turmeric, onion powder, and chopped onion.
2. Set aside to marinate for a few minutes.
3. In a separate bowl, toss the potatoes in the olive oil, and air fry at 400 degrees Fahrenheit for 15 minutes, checking and shaking at around the 7-8 minute mark to ensure even cooking.
4. Shake the potatoes again, add the tofu (reserving any leftover marinade) and cook at 370 degrees Fahrenheit for 15 more minutes.
5. Toss the broccoli in the reserved marinade, adding extra soy sauce if the marinade is not enough, 5 minutes towards the end of cooking, add the broccoli to the air fryer and shake the basket to combine all the ingredients.
6. Once done, serve and enjoy!

Granola Bars

Servings: 6
Total Time: 18 Minutes
Ingredients and Quantity
- 9 oz. gluten-free rolled oats
- 1 oz. light brown sugar
- 1 medium peeled, cooked apple
- 3 oz. melted vegan butter
- 3 tbsp. maple syrup
- 1 tbsp. olive oil
- 1 tsp. ground cinnamon
- 1 tsp. vanilla extract
- A handful raisins

Direction
1. In a blender, blend the gluten-free oats into a flour and then add in all the rest of the dry ingredients.
2. In the air fryer baking pan, add, with a small wooden spoon stir all the wet ingredients well.
3. Pour all the dry ingredients into the wet and mix well with a fork.
4. Then add the raisins and press down on the mixture into the baking pan and make sure all the ingredients are all level.
5. Cook at 320 degrees Fahrenheit for 10 minutes in the air fryer, followed by another 5 minutes at 360 degrees Fahrenheit.
6. Once cooked, remove the granola and place the baking pan in the freezer for 5 minutes to stiffen them up.
7. Slice into granola bars and serve. Enjoy!

Oat, Sunflower, Pecan and Raisin Granola

Servings: 5
Total Time: 10 Minutes
Ingredients and Quantity
- 1 1/2 cups rolled oats
- 3 tbsp. real maple syrup
- 2 tbsp. vegan butter, melted
- 1/2 cup pecans, roughly chopped
- 1/2 cup sunflower seeds
- 1/2 cup raisins
- 1/2 tsp. salt

Direction
1. Add all the ingredients except for the butter, maple syrup, and 1/2 of the raisins into a bowl.
2. Then add the maple syrup and melted butter and mix thoroughly.
3. Line the air fryer basket with aluminum foil and preheat the air fryer to 180 degrees Celsius.
4. Cook the mixture for 3 minutes and then take out and stir well.
5. Air fry again for a further 2 minutes and then pour the granola mixture into a tray to cool.
6. While the granola cools, add the remaining raisins.
7. Top your oats or cereal with the granola and enjoy!

Sweet Rosemary Cornbread

Servings: 4
Total Time: 30 Minutes
Ingredients and Quantity

- 1/4 cup fine or medium ground yellow cornmeal
- 1/2 cup sorghum flour
- 1 cup plain soy, almond or other non-dairy milk
- 1/2 cup vegan butter, softened
- 1/4 cup granulated sugar
- 1/4 cup tapioca
- 3 tbsp. olive oil
- 2 tsp. fresh minced rosemary
- 2 tsp. baking powder
- 1/2 tsp. xanthan gum
- 1/4 tsp. fine sea salt
- Agave nectar, to taste

Direction

1. Lightly grease a ceramic ramekin with cooking oil spray.
2. In a large bowl, mix together the yellow cornmeal, sorghum flour, tapioca, sugar, xantham gum, baking powder, and salt.
3. Add the soymilk (or other plant-based milk), olive oil and fresh rosemary to the flour mixture, whisking well until mixed.
4. Scoop the batter into the prepared ceramic ramekins.
5. Bake at 375 – 400 degrees Fahrenheit for 15 to 20 minutes in the air fryer.
6. Note that the baking times will vary depending on the size of the ramekins you use and also the model of air fryer used.
7. Once done, the cornbread should be lightly browned on top, firm to the touch and a cake tester inserted into the center should come out clean.
8. In a small bowl, mix together butter and 2 tablespoons agave nectar until smooth.
9. Remove the cornbread from air fryer and set aside to cool.
10. Serve with agave butter. Enjoy!

Corn Muffins

Servings: 12
Total Time: 17 Minutes
Ingredients and Quantity

- 1 packet corn mix
- 1 flax egg
- 1/3 cup almond milk

Direction

1. In a medium-sized bowl mix the corn mix, flax egg and almond milk until smooth.
2. Pour the muffin mix into a greased muffin tin or muffin silicone holders, and air fry at 320 degrees Fahrenheit, for 12 minutes.
3. When done, serve immediately, warm and enjoy!

Lunch Recipes

Vegan Balls

Servings: 6
Total Time: 40 Minutes
Ingredients and Quantity

- 1/2 cup desiccated coconut
- 1 cup gluten-free oats
- 1 tsp. chives
- 1 tsp. mixed spice
- 1 tsp. paprika
- 100 g sweet potato
- 2 tsp. garlic puree
- 2 tsp. oregano
- 200 g cauliflower
- 70 g carrots
- 90g parsnips
- Salt and pepper, to taste

Direction

1. Put the raw vegetables into food processor and process until the mixture resembles breadcrumbs.
2. Put the processed veggie mixture into a tea towel and wring out excess liquid – this will help keep the meatballs firm.
3. Transfer to a mixing bowl. Add the rest of the ingredients and mix until well combined.
4. Form the mixture into medium-sized balls.
5. Put the balls in the fridge and let freeze for 2 hours so that they can firm up.
6. Put the balls in the air fryer basket.
7. Set the temperature to 160C and set the timer for 10 minutes. After 10 minutes, turn the balls.
8. Set the temperature to 200C and the timer for 10 minutes. Serve and enjoy!
9. Note: If the meatball mixture is not sticking well enough to form into balls, add a little bit more oats to stiffen it – apply the oats accordingly.

Avocado Fries

Servings: 3
Total Time: 20 Minutes
Ingredients and Quantity

- 1 Hass avocado, peeled, pitted and sliced
- 1/2 cup panko breadcrumbs
- 1/2 tsp. salt
- Aquafaba from 1 can (15 oz.) garbanzo beans or white beans

Direction

1. Put the salt and panko breadcrumbs into a shallow bowl and toss to mix.
2. Dredge the slices of avocado in the aquafaba and then coat with the panko mixture, covering them evenly well.
3. In a single layer, arrange the coated slices in the air fryer basket – DO NOT OVERLAP.
4. Set the temperature to 390F and the timer for 10 minutes. Shake well after 5 minutes.
5. Serve right away with your favorite vegan dipping sauce. Enjoy!

Vegan Bacon Wrapped Mini Breakfast Burritos

Servings: 4
Total Time: 30 Minutes
Ingredients and Quantity
- 1 to 2 tbsp. liquid smoke
- 1 to 2 tbsp. water
- 2 servings of your favorite tofu scramble or vegan scramble
- 2 tbsp. cashew butter
- 2 to 3 tbsp. tamari
- 4 pieces rice paper

For the Vegetable Add-ins:
- 8 strips roasted red pepper
- 6 to 8 stalks fresh asparagus
- 1 small tree broccoli, sautéed
- 1/3 cup roasted sweet potato cubes
- Handful kale, spinach and/or other grains

Direction
1. Put the water, liquid smoke, tamari, and cashew butter in a small-sized, shallow bowl and whisk to combine. Set aside.
2. Make ready a clean surface or a large-sized plate for filling and rolling the rice paper.
3. Hold a sheet of rice paper under the faucet of cool running water, wetting both the sides of the wrapper for a couple of seconds until wet – the rice papers will soften more as it sits, but they will not get too soft that they will stick onto a surface or rip when you handle them.
4. Put the filling just in the middle of the sheet, leaving the sides free.
5. Fold the 2 sides, folding it like a burrito, roll into a log, and seal.
6. Dip the roll in the cashew butter mixture, completely coating it.
7. Put the roll onto a parchment paper-lined baking sheet.
8. Repeat the process with the remaining rolls filling and rice paper sheet.
9. Set the temperature to 350 F and the timer to 8 to 10 minutes, or till the rice papers are crispy. Serve and enjoy!

Fried Sweet Potato and Homemade Guacamole

Servings: 2
Total Time: 45 Minutes
Ingredients and Quantity
For the Fries:
- 1 to 2 sweet potatoes, medium-sized, washed and peel left on
- 1 tbsp. coconut oil, melted

For the Guacamole:
- 1 bunch fresh herbs, roughly chopped, I used rosemary, oregano and parsley
- 1 ripe avocado, large-sized
- 1 medium-size cucumber, sliced and diced
- 1 medium-size tomato, sliced and diced
- 1 tsp. garlic powder
- Himalayan pink salt, to taste
- Pepper, to taste

Direction
1. For the fries: Slice the sweet potatoes lengthwise into long-shaped pieces and then put them in a mixing bowl.
2. Add the coconut oil and toss to coat.
3. Put into the air fryer basket.
4. Set the temperature to 375F or 190C and set the timer for 20-30 minutes or until cooked and golden – shake halfway through cooking.
5. When the fries are cooked, transfer to a serving platter or serving bowl and sprinkle with additional salt.
6. Serve with the guacamole.
7. For the guacamole: While the sweet potato fries are baking, prepare all the ingredients as described above.
8. Slice the avocado into halves; discard the seeds and pith.
9. Put the avocado meat in a mixing bowl and mash to desired consistency.
10. Add the rest of the ingredients and stir to combine.
11. Refrigerate until the fries are cooked. Serve and enjoy!

Corn Tortilla Chips

Servings: 2
Total Time: 4 Minutes
Ingredients and Quantity
- 8 corn tortillas
- 1 tbsp. olive oil
- Salt, to taste

Direction
1. Preheat the air fryer to 200C.
2. Using a sharp knife, slice the corn tortillas into triangles.
3. Brush all the triangles with the olive oil.
4. Put half the tortilla pieces in the air fryer basket and set the timer for 3 minutes.
5. Repeat the process with the remaining half.
6. Sprinkle the cooked tortilla with the salt.
7. Serve with salsa, guacamole, or your preferred dip. Enjoy!

Crispy Vegetable Fries

Servings: 4
Total Time: 23 Minutes
Ingredients and Quantity
- 1 cup panko breadcrumbs (regular or gluten-free)
- 1 cup rice flour
- 2 tbsp. vegan egg powder (I used Follow Your Heart)
- 2 tbsp. nutritional yeast flakes, divided
- 2/3 cup cold water
- Assorted veggies of your choice, sliced into shapes similar to French fry or into bite-size chunks (such as green beans, cauliflower, zucchini, sweet onions or squash)
- Salt and pepper

Direction
1. Prepare 3 pieces of shallow dishes on a counter.
2. Put rice flour in one of the dishes.
3. In the second dish, whisk the egg powder with 2/3 cup water and 1 tbsp. nutritional yeast until the mixture is smooth.
4. In the third dish, mix the panko breadcrumbs with the remaining 1 tbsp. nutritional yeast and then add a couple pinches of pepper and salt.
5. Working one vegetable piece at a time, coat with rice flour, into the vegan egg mixture, and finally in the breadcrumb mix, pressing to set the coating. Prepare as many veggies as you desire.
6. Lightly spritz the air fryer with oil.
7. Alternatively, you can line the air fryer basket with parchment paper that is smaller than the basket.
8. Carefully put the coated veggies in the air fryer basket and gently spritz with oil.
9. Set the temperature to 380F and the timer for 8 minutes.
10. Cook for additional minutes, if needed.
11. Serve while still crispy and hot with your choice of dipping sauce. Enjoy!

Buffalo Cauliflower

Servings: 4
Total Time: 30 Minutes
Ingredients and Quantity
For the Cauliflower:
- 4 cups cauliflower - use florets that are in the size of 2 pieces baby carrots put side-by-side
- 1 cup panko breadcrumbs
- 1 tsp. sea salt - Do not use regular salt

For the Buffalo Coating:
- 1/4 cup vegan Buffalo sauce (I used Frank's Red Hot) - check the ingredients for butter
- 1/4 cup vegan butter, melted measurement

For Dipping:
- Vegan mayo cashew ranch, or your favorite creamy salad dressing

Direction
1. Put the vegan butter in a microwavable mug and microwave to melt. Add the buffalo sauce and whisk to combine.
2. Combine the panko breadcrumbs with the salt in a shallow bowl.
3. Hold a floret by the stem, dip into the Buffalo coating, making sure that the floret is coated with the sauce – it's perfectly fine if the stem isn't coated with the sauce.
4. Hold the floret over the mug until the sauce stops dripping from it – few drips are okay, but the raining sauce is not since it will make the panko bread clumpy and stop sticking on the cauliflower.
5. Dredge the sauce-coated floret in the breadcrumb mixture, coating it as much as you like, and then put into the air fryer basket.
6. Repeat the process with the remaining florets – no need to arrange them in a single layer in the basket, just put them in.
7. Set the temperature to 350F and set the timer for 14-17 minutes, shaking the basket a couple of times and checking the progress during the process. The cauliflower is cooked when the florets are browned a little bit.
8. Serve with your choice of dipping sauce. Enjoy!

Dinner Recipes

Cauliflower Chickpea Tacos

Servings: 4
Total Time: 30 Minutes
Ingredients and Quantity

- 19 oz. can chickpeas, drained and rinsed
- 4 cups cauliflower florets, cut into bite-sized pieces
- 2 tbsp. taco seasoning
- 2 tbsp. olive oil

For Serving:

- 8 small flour tortillas
- 4 cups cabbage, finely shredded
- 2 Haas avocados, sliced
- Coconut yogurt, for drizzling

Direction

1. Pre-heat the air fryer to 390 degrees Fahrenheit.
2. In a large bowl, toss the chickpeas and cauliflower with taco seasoning and olive oil.
3. Put them into the basket of the air fryer and cook in the air fryer for 20 minutes. Make sure to check occasionally to ensure the cauliflower and chickpeas are evenly cooked through.
4. Serve in tacos with the cabbage, avocado slices, and coconut yogurt drizzled on top. Enjoy!

Spicy Cauliflower Stir Fry

Servings: 4
Total Time: 30 Minutes
Calories: 93
Fat: 3 g
Protein: 4 g
Carbs: 12 g
Fiber: 1.2 g
Ingredients and Quantity

- 1 head cauliflower, cut into florets
- 5 garlic cloves, finely sliced
- 3/4 cup Spanish onion, thinly sliced
- 1 1/2 tbsp. tamari, gluten-free tamari or light soy sauce
- 1 tbsp. sriracha or any other of your favorite hot sauces
- 1 tbsp. rice vinegar
- 1/2 tsp. coconut sugar

For Garnishing:

- 2 scallions, sliced

Direction

1. Place the cauliflower in the air fryer. If the air fryer has holes in the bottom, you will need to use an additional air fryer insert.
2. Preheat the air fryer to 350 degrees Fahrenheit and cook for 10 minutes.
3. Open the air fryer, remove and shake the insert and slide back in to the compartment.
4. Add the sliced white onion, stir and cook for a further 10 minutes.
5. Add the garlic, and stir and cook for 5 more minutes.
6. Then in a small bowl, mix the rice vinegar, soy sauce, coconut sugar, Sriracha hot sauce, salt and pepper.
7. Add in the mixture to the cauliflower in the air fryer and stir.
8. Cook for a further 5 minutes. The insert will keep all of the juices inside.
9. Transfer to a serving bowl and sprinkle the sliced scallions over the top to garnish. Enjoy!

Orange Tofu

Servings: 4
Total Time: 40 Minutes
Calories: 109
Fat: 3 g
Protein: 8 g
Carbs: 11 g
Fiber: 2 g

Ingredients and Quantity

For the Tofu:
- 1 lb. extra-firm tofu, drained and pressed
- 1 tbsp. tamari
- 1 tbsp. cornstarch or arrowroot powder

For the Sauce:
- 1 tsp. fresh ginger, minced
- 1 tsp. fresh garlic, minced
- 1 tsp. orange zest
- 1/3 cup orange juice
- 1/2 cup water
- 2 tsp. cornstarch or arrowroot powder
- 1 tbsp. real maple syrup
- 1/4 tsp. red pepper flakes

Direction

1. Cut the tofu into 1-inch cubes.
2. Place the tofu in a Ziploc bag and add the tamari then seal the bag. Shake the bag until all the tofu is well coated with the tamari.
3. Now add the tablespoon of cornstarch to the bag and shake again until all the tofu is coated. Marinate for 15 minutes or more.
4. Now add all the sauce ingredients to a small bowl and mix well.
5. In a single layer, place the tofu into the air fryer and cook the tofu at 390 degrees Fahrenheit for 10 minutes, shaking it halfway through cooking. The tofu will probably need to be cooked in batches to avoid uneven cooking.
6. Once done, add the tofu to a skillet on the stove top over a medium-high heat.
7. Stir the sauce and pour it over the tofu until the sauce is thick and glossy and the tofu is heated through.
8. Serve immediately with rice, noodles and steamed vegetables, if desired. Enjoy!

Southern Fried Chicken Soy Curls

Servings: 2
Total Time: 25 Minutes
Calories: 100
Fat: 1 g
Protein: 4 g
Carbs: 17 g
Fiber: 3 g
Ingredients and Quantity
- 4 oz. (1/2 bag) soy curls
- 3 cups boiling water

For the Breading:
- 1/4 cup fine ground cornmeal (it can be substituted with flour)
- 1/4 cup nutritional yeast
- 1 tsp. poultry seasoning
- 1 to 2 tsp. Cajun seasoning
- Salt and pepper, to taste

Direction
1. Put the soy curls into a heat-proof pan on the stovetop and pour boiling water over the curls.
2. Let the curls soak for 5 - 10 minutes, or until rehydrated and plump.
3. Drain the tofu and press out the extra water with a spoon.
4. Mix all the breading ingredients in a small bowl.
5. Add the drained soy curls to a large bowl and mix with the breading. Each piece should be well coated.
6. Place the breaded soy curls into the air fryer and cook at 380 degrees Fahrenheit for 5 minutes. At this point, shake well and cook for a further 5 minutes.
7. Serve as is with fries, over mashed potatoes or with a gravy. Enjoy!

Golden Turmeric Cauliflower Steaks

Servings: 2
Total Time: 25 Minutes
Ingredients and Quantity
- 1 to 2 medium heads cauliflower, stems intact
- 2 tbsp. coconut oil or coconut spray oil
- 1 tsp. ground turmeric
- 1/4 tsp. ground ginger
- 1/8 tsp. ground cumin
- 1/8 tsp. salt
- A pinch black pepper

For Serving:
- Mixed steamed greens
- Tahini
- White sesame seeds

Direction
1. Cut the cauliflower head down the middle, leaving the stem intact. Trim off any green leaves.
2. On either side of the half, cut 1-inch steaks taking care not to make them too thin. Reserve any fallen florets for use at a later date.
3. Coat the steaks with coconut oil or coconut oil spray and rub the spices into all of the cracks and crevices of the cauliflower.
4. This recipes can be prepared in the oven or in an air fryer. Cook at 390 degrees Fahrenheit for about 15 minutes, turning over the steaks halfway through the cooking time.
5. Serve on a bed of mixed greens drizzled with tahini.
6. Garnish with white sesame seeds, if desired. Enjoy!

Portobello Mushrooms with Hummus Sauce

Servings: 4
Total Time: 25 Minutes
Calories: 70
Fat: 1.6 g
Protein: 4.3 g
Carbs: 11 g
Fiber: 3.5 g

Ingredients and Quantity

- 4 large Portobello mushrooms
- 4 tbsp. oil-free pasta sauce
- 1 garlic clove, minced
- 2 tbsp. red bell pepper, diced
- 1/2 cup hummus
- 3 oz. zucchini, grated
- 4 olives Kalamata olives, pitted and sliced
- 1 tsp. dried basil
- Balsamic vinegar
- Salt and black pepper, to taste
- Fresh basil leaves or other herbs, finely chopped

Direction

1. Wash the Portobello mushrooms, cut off the stems and remove the grills. Pat the insides dry and brush both sides with balsamic vinegar.
2. Season the mushrooms with salt and pepper.
3. Spread 1 tablespoon of the pasta sauce inside each mushroom and sprinkle with the chopped garlic.
4. Preheat the air fryer to 330degrees Fahrenheit.
5. Place the mushrooms in a single layer and cook for 3 minutes.
6. Remove the mushrooms and top each with equal portions of peppers, zucchini and olives and sprinkle with dried basil, salt and pepper.
7. Return the mushrooms to the air fryer and cook for 3 more minutes.
8. Check the mushrooms after 3 minutes and return to the air fryer for another 3 minutes or until mushrooms are tender.
9. Place on a plate, drizzle with hummus and sprinkle with the fresh basil or any other herb of your choice.
10. Serve immediately. Enjoy!

Red Bean Chipotle Burgers

Servings: 6
Total Time: 40 Minutes
Calories: 124
Fat: 1 g
Protein: 6 g
Carbs: 24 g
Fiber: 4 g

Ingredients and Quantity
- 1 small white onion, peeled and quartered
- 1 garlic cloves, minced
- One 16 oz. can kidney beans, drained and rinsed
- 1/2 cup cooked brown rice
- 1/2 cup old-fashioned or quick oats, uncooked
- 1 to 3 tsp. chopped canned chipotles,
- 1/2 to 2 tsp. chipotle chili powder, or hot smoked paprika, to taste
- 1 tbsp. tomato paste
- 1/2 tsp. thyme
- 1/2 tsp. oregano
- 1/2 tsp. salt (optional to make the recipe salt-free)

Direction
1. Put the garlic and onion into a food processor and pulse to a coarse consistency.
2. Add the beans and process until they are coarsely chopped.
3. Then add the remaining ingredients and process until well blended but not to a smooth paste; it should be the consistency of ground beef.
4. Preheat the air fryer to 390 degrees Fahrenheit.
5. Form the burgers on baking parchment paper and transfer to the air fryer.
6. Cook for 8 minutes.
7. Turn the burgers over and rearrange from top to bottom if you are using a rack.
8. Cook for 4-8 more minutes, until the burgers are crispy outside and firm inside. Do not overcook or they will come out too hard.
9. Serve with fries and the dipping sauce of your choice. Enjoy!

Crisp Banana Chips

Servings: 2
Total Time: 18 Minutes

Ingredients and Quantity
- 1 large-sized plantain banana
- 1 tsp. coconut oil
- 1/2 tsp. salt
- 1/4 tsp. turmeric powder
- Pinch chili powder

Direction
1. Preheat the air fryer to 190C.
2. Peel the plantain and cut it into thin round pieces - do not slice them into wafer thin pieces, otherwise, the chips will fly into the coils when they begin to get crispy.
3. Put the plantain slices into a bowl and toss with the turmeric powder and coconut oil.
4. Transfer to the air fryer basket and set the timer for 7 to 8 minutes, removing and shaking the basket every 2 minutes. The chips are done when they are crisp and light golden brown.
5. When the chips are cooked, let them cool 2 minutes or more to allow them to get crisper. Serve and enjoy!

Whole Wheat Eggless Chocolate Chips Cookies

Servings: 6
Total Time: 50 Minutes
Ingredients and Quantity
- 1 cup whole-wheat flour
- 1/2 to 3/4 cup powdered sugar or castor sugar
- 1/2 cup unsalted butter (I used I Can't Believe It's Not Butter)
- 1/4 baking powder
- 2 tsp. nut milk
- 2 tsp. vegan chocolate chips (I used Enjoy Life)

Direction
1. Put the baking powder, flour, and butter in a mixing bowl. With your fingers, rub the ingredients together until the mixture resembles breadcrumbs.
2. Add the milk, sugar, and chocolate chips. Mix to incorporate – the dough should be soft but firm.
3. Refrigerate 15 to 20 minutes.
4. When the dough is firm, form into balls and then flatten into cookie shapes. If desired, you can use a cookie cutter to shape them.
5. Glaze the top of the cookies with a bit of milk.
6. Put the cookie doughs into a preheated 160 C air fryer for 10 minutes. Set the timer to 10 minutes cooking.
7. When the timer beeps, let it sit on standby mode for 10 minutes, allowing the cookies to cool inside the air fryer.
8. Store leftovers in an airtight container. Serve and enjoy!

Seaweed Salad with Crispy Tofu and Veggies

Servings: 4
Total Time: 53 Minutes
Ingredients and Quantity
- 1 batch of crispy tofu (starch the tofu once the wakame is on the stove)
- 1 cucumber, large-sized
- 1 Hass avocado, chopped
- 1/4 cup green onion, chopped
- 1/4 cup sesame seeds
- 1/4 cup shiitake sesame vinaigrette (I used Annie's Naturals)
- 2 carrots, peeled
- 3 strips of dried wakame

Direction
1. Soak the wakame in water for 5 minutes.
2. After soaking, drain and then chop the strips into the bite-sized piece.
3. Boil a pot of water.
4. When the water is boiling, put the wakame pieces and boil for 5 minutes. After boiling, drain the wakame pieces and put in the refrigerator to chill.
5. Spiralize the carrots and cucumber. If you do not have a sriracha, then just chop them.
6. Toss the cucumber and carrots with the chilled wakame.
7. Top with the tofu, avocado, green onion and sesame seeds. Serve and enjoy!

Thai-Inspired Barbecue Cauliflower

Servings: 4
Total Time: 48 Minutes
Ingredients and Quantity
- 1 large or 2 small head cauliflower
- 1 lemon, zest only
- 1 lime, zest only
- 1 tbsp. brown sugar
- 1/2 cup pumpkin seeds
- 10 garlic cloves
- 1 to 2 tbsp. sriracha
- 2 tbsp. curry powder
- 3 tbsp. arrowroot starch or cornstarch
- 3/4 cup coconut milk
- Hot rice, for serving
- Raw vegetables, for serving, optional
- Sea salt, to taste

Direction
1. Put the curry, cornstarch, garlic, milk, zest, sugar, sriracha, and salt to taste into a small-sized blender, and then blend until the mixture smooth.
2. Cut the cauliflower into florets and put into a large-sized bowl.
3. Add the curry mixture, toss to coat well, and let marinate for 10 minutes.
4. Put 1/2 of the marinated cauliflower into the air fryer basket.
5. Set the temperature to 360F and set the timer for 15 minutes, basting every 5 minutes.
6. Adjust the temperature to 390 F, set the timer for 5 to 8 minutes, and cook until crisp.
7. When they are only 2 minutes of cooking, add 1/2 of the pumpkin seeds in the air fryer.
8. Repeat the processor with the remaining marinated cauliflower and pumpkin seeds.
9. Serve with raw vegies, such as celery sticks and carrots, or with hot rice. Serve and enjoy!

Main Dish Recipes

Spiced Crusted Tofu

Servings: 4
Total Time: 6 Minutes
Ingredients and Quantity

- One 20 oz. container high-protein tofu or super firm tofu, cut into cubes
- 1 tsp. ground chili powder (reduce if you prefer it milder)
- 1 tsp. ground cumin powder
- 1/2 tsp. smoked paprika
- 1/4 tsp. salt, or to taste

Direction

1. Coat the tofu cubes with the chili powder, smoked paprika, cumin and salt.
2. Preheat the air fryer to 390 degrees Fahrenheit. Once it's hot, add the coated tofu to the air fryer basket.
3. Cook for 5 minutes and when the cook time is up, shake or stir the tofu.
4. Repeat for a further 5 minutes.
5. Once done, serve immediately. Enjoy!

Thai Crab Cakes

Servings: 8
Total Time: 35 Minutes
Calories: 97
Fat: 0.4 g
Protein: 4 g
Carbs: 20 g
Fiber: 2 g
Ingredients and Quantity

- 4 cups (4 medium) diced potatoes
- 1 1/2 inches knob fresh ginger
- 1 bunch green onions, sliced
- 1 tbsp. soy sauce or tamari
- 4 tbsp. Thai red curry paste
- 1 can long, tubular hearts palm, the long tubular
- 1 lime, juice and zest
- 4 sheets nori
- 3/4 cup canned artichoke hearts
- Pepper, to taste
- Salt, to taste
- 2 tbsp. oil, for frying (optional)

Direction

1. Peel and dice the potatoes then add them to a pan.
2. Cover with water and boil on the stove top until they are fork tender and then drain, mash and set aside.
3. While the potatoes are boiling, add the green onions, lime zest, lime juice, ginger, tamari (or soy sauce) and curry paste to a food processor.
4. Break the nori sheets into manageable pieces and put them in the food processor with all the other ingredients. Process until it becomes a smooth paste. The nori will stay a little chunkier.
5. Drain the hearts of palm and grate them, or alternatively shred them with a fork.
6. Drain the artichokes and roughly chop them. Be sure to drain them thoroughly and also to give the artichokes a little squeeze to get any extra liquid out of them.
7. Once the potatoes are cool, add the paste and stir through so it's evenly distributed, then add the hearts of palm and the chopped artichoke and then gently stir through.
8. Form the mixture into patties and place them on a tray lined with baking parchment.
9. Air fry at 380 degrees Fahrenheit for 15 minutes.
10. Serve immediately. Enjoy!
11. Note: Once shaped, the cake can be stored in a fridge uncooked for 2 to 3 days. For leftovers, reheat well in the oven.

Black Bean Burgers

Servings: 6
Total Time: 35 Minutes
Calories: 158
Fat: 1.3 g
Protein: 8 g
Carbs: 30 g
Fiber: 9 g

Ingredients and Quantity

- 1/2 cup corn kernels (fresh or frozen and thawed work well)
- One 16 oz. can black beans, drained and rinsed
- 1 1/3 cups gluten-free rolled oats
- 3/4 cup salsa
- 1 tbsp. soy sauce
- 1/4 to 1/2 tsp. chipotle chili powder, or to taste
- 1 1/4 tsp. mild chili powder
- 1/2 tsp. garlic powder

Direction

1. Place the oats in a food processor fitted with an S-blade.
2. Pulse 5 to 6 times until they are partially chopped and then add all the ingredients except the corn, then pulse until most of the beans are blended.
3. Pour the bean mixture into a bowl and stir in the corn kernels. Cover and refrigerate for 15 minutes.
4. Preheat the air fryer to 375 degrees Fahrenheit.
5. Place the burgers in a single layer, on baking parchment paper, into the air fryer and cook until slightly crispy on the outside; this takes about 15 minutes.
6. **Note:** These burgers are easily frozen either baked or unbaked. Shape the burgers and wrap them to store in the freezer for up to 3 months. Thaw the unbaked burgers well before cooking.

Cheesy Vegan Quesaritos

Servings: 1
Total Time: 15 Minutes
Ingredients and Quantity

- 2 large gluten-free tortillas
- 3 to 4 tbsp. cooked Spanish rice
- 4 tbsp. vegan Queso Fresco, divided into 2 portions
- 3 tbsp. meaty crumbles
- 2 to 3 tbsp. grated vegan cheese
- 1 tbsp. cashew cream
- 1 to 2 tbsp. chipotle cream

Extras:

- Fresh baby spinach
- Fresh bell peppers
- Roasted red peppers

Direction
1. Lay a tortilla flat on a clean prep surface.
2. Using a knife, carefully cut an inch from the entire edge of the second tortilla, making one smaller tortilla and then set aside.
3. On the first tortilla, spread the vegan Queso fresco cheese around the middle in a circle the size of the smaller tortilla.
4. Add about 3 tablespoons of grated cheese to the top of the Queso fresco cheese, in an even layer across the small circle, reserving 1 tablespoon of grated cheese.
5. Top the Queso fresco cheese circle with the smaller second tortilla, pressing down gently.
6. Onto the middle of the second smaller tortilla, spoon a line of meaty crumbles, Spanish rice and cashew cream.
7. Carefully fold and roll the burrito tightly.
8. Secure the edge with the reserved 1 tablespoon of grated cheese. This cheese will melt and seal the burrito.
9. Place the burrito sealed side down into the air fryer basket.
10. Crisp in the air fryer at 370 degrees Fahrenheit for 6 - 7 minutes until lightly golden and crisp.
11. Serve immediately. Enjoy!

Whiskey Garlic Tofu with Veggie Quinoa

Servings: 2
Total Time: 20 Minutes
Ingredients and Quantity

- 1 block extra firm tofu, pressed
- 1/4 cup vegan coconut or maple sugar
- 1/4 cup whiskey or bourbon
- 1 tbsp. apple cider vinegar
- 2 garlic cloves, finely minced
- 1 tsp. onion powder
- Sea salt and black pepper, to taste

Direction
1. If using an air fryer, line the basket with a round of baking parchment paper.
2. Once the tofu is pressed, sliced it into half inch slabs.
3. In saucepan, combine the vegan sugar, whiskey or bourbon, garlic, vinegar and onion powder.
4. Stir continually, bringing to a boil, then reduce to a simmer. Simmer for about 10 minutes, stirring constantly.
5. Allow to cool.
6. Coat all the tofu slices and place on a baking sheet lined with baking parchment paper.
7. Fry in the air fryer at 370 degrees Fahrenheit for 7 minutes.
8. Turn the tofu over and cook another 3-4 minutes.
9. Serve over salad, mashed potatoes or with veggie quinoa. Enjoy!

Special Noodles

Servings: 1
Total Time: 10 Minutes
Ingredients and Quantity
- 1 to 2 vegetables that can be spiralized. Use squash, potatoes, zucchini or sweet potatoes.

Direction
1. Using a spiral slicer, cut the vegetable into noodles.
2. Add the veggie noodles to the air fryer and cook at 350 degrees Fahrenheit, for about 5 minutes, tossing about every minute or so.
3. The noodles may take more or less time, but should be removed when they are springy and al dente.
4. Remove from the air-fryer, and toss with your favorite noodle sauce. Serve and enjoy!

BBQ Soy Curls

Servings: 2
Total Time: 21 Minutes
Ingredients and Quantity
- 1 cup soy curls
- 1 cup warm water
- 1 tsp. canola oil
- 1 tsp. vegetarian stock base
- 1/4 cup BBQ sauce

Direction
1. Air fry the soy curls at 400 degrees Fahrenheit for 3 minutes. Work in batches to prevent overcrowding and to allow the curls to crisp up properly.
2. Remove the soy curls put them back to the mixing bowl, toss in BBQ sauce and stir.
3. Make sure all of the curls get coated.
4. Return to air fryer and cook at 400 degrees Fahrenheit for 5 minutes stopping twice to shake the pan.
5. Serve the curls with a vegan potato salad, mixed greens, and also a non-dairy mac and cheese. Enjoy!

Rainbow Veggies

Servings: 4
Total Time: 30 Minutes
Calories: 69
Fat: 3.8 g
Protein: 2.6 g
Carbs: 7.7 g
Fiber: 2.5 g
Ingredients and Quantity
- 1 zucchini, finely diced
- 1 red bell pepper, seeded and diced
- 1 yellow summer squash, finely diced
- 1/2 sweet white onion, finely diced
- 4 oz. fresh mushrooms, cleaned and halved
- 1 tbsp. extra-virgin olive oil
- Salt and pepper, to taste

Direction
1. Preheat the air fryer according to the recommendations of the air fryer.
2. Place the red bell pepper, zucchini, mushrooms, squash and onion in a large bowl.
3. Add the olive oil, black pepper and salt, and toss to combine.
4. Place the vegetables in a single layer in the air fryer basket.
5. Air-fry the vegetables for 20 minutes, stirring halfway through the cooking time. Serve and enjoy!

5 Spice Tofu

Servings: 4
Total Time: 30 Minutes
Ingredients and Quantity
- One 12 oz. block extra-firm tofu
- 2 tbsp. oil

For the Marinade:
- 1 tbsp. Chinese black vinegar plus 1 tsp.
- 2 tsp. Chinese five spice powder
- 2 tsp. garlic powder
- 1 tsp. dark soy sauce
- 1/4 cup maple syrup
- 1/2 tsp. salt or to taste

Direction
1. Mix the marinade ingredients in a large bowl.
2. Drain the tofu.
3. Wrap up the tofu in a clean kitchen paper towel and squeeze to remove excess water.
4. This will cause the tofu to crumble into chunks.
5. Add the tofu to the marinade and mix until all the marinade is well absorbed.
6. Drizzle the oil over the tofu and mix.
7. Prepare the air fryer basket by spraying it with cooking oil spray. This will ensure the tofu doesn't stick.
8. Transfer the tofu to the air fryer basket and cook at 400 degrees Fahrenheit for 20 minutes, shaking the basket halfway through cooking.
9. Serve piping hot. Enjoy!

Crumbed Tempeh

Servings: 2
Total Time: 17 Minutes
Ingredients and Quantity
- 200g packet tempeh
- 3 to 4 tbsp. Besan flour
- 1/2 tsp. celery salt
- 1 tsp. smoked paprika
- 1/2 cup Panko breadcrumbs
- Almond milk

Direction
1. Slice up the tempeh in 1cm strips.
2. Mix the Besan flour, celery salt and paprika.
3. Dip the tempeh strip into the almond milk then coat with the flour mix.
4. Put the tempeh back into the milk and then coat with the breadcrumbs.
5. Sprinkle a little extra celery salt and cook at 180 degrees Celsius for 12 minutes. Serve and enjoy!

Buffalo Tofu

Servings: 2
Total Time: 1 Hour 20 Minutes
Ingredients and Quantity
- 1 block extra-firm tofu, drained and pressed
- 1 cup hot sauce
- 1/4 cup vegan butter, melted

For Serving:
- Vegan ranch or blue cheese dressing

Direction
1. Cut the tofu into squares.
2. Preheat the air fryer to 390 degrees Fahrenheit.
3. Whisk the hot sauce with the melted butter to form the buffalo sauce.
4. Marinate the tofu in the buffalo sauce mixture for 30 - 60 minutes.
5. Once the air fryer is preheated, coat the basket lightly with cooking oil spray and using tongs, add the tofu to the air fryer basket. Reserve the marinade.
6. Air-fry for 20 - 30 minutes, checking and shaking the tofu after 10 minutes, and then each additional 5 minutes after that.
7. Check the tofu each time for the desired crispness.
8. Toss the tofu back into the reserved hot sauce and then transfer to a serving plate.
9. If desired, serve alongside vegan blue cheese or ranch dressing. Enjoy!

Sides And Snacks Recipes

Bow Tie Pasta Chips

Servings: 6
Total Time: 25 Minutes
Ingredients and Quantity

- 2 cups dry whole-wheat, gluten-free bow tie pasta
- 1 tbsp. nutritional yeast
- 1 tbsp. olive oil
- 1 1/2 tsp. Italian seasoning
- 1/2 tsp. salt

Direction

1. Par-cook the pasta for half the time detailed on the packet instructions.
2. Toss the drained pasta in the olive oil, nutritional yeast, Italian seasoning and salt.
3. Place about half of the mixture into the air fryer basket in order to cook in 2 batches; larger air fryers may be able to cook all the pasta in one batch.
4. Cook at 390 degrees Fahrenheit for 5 minutes.
5. Shake the basket and cook for 3 - 5 minutes more or until crunchy and crisp.
6. Serve immediately. Enjoy!
7. Note that these pasta chips will crisp up as they cool. You may store left overs in an airtight container for up to 2 days.

Garlic Parmesan Chips

Servings: 5
Total Time: 60 Minutes
Ingredients and Quantity

- 2 large red waxy potatoes
- 4 garlic cloves, minced
- 2 tbsp. vegan parmesan
- 2 tsp. salt

Direction

1. Thinly slice the potatoes using a 1.5mm mandolin blade.
2. Place the sliced potatoes in a bowl filled with salted water and soak for 30 minutes.
3. Drain and rinse the potatoes.
4. Pat with a kitchen paper towel to dry.
5. Toss the potatoes with the minced garlic and vegan parmesan.
6. Layer half the potato slices in the air fryer basket, in no more than 4 or so layers.
7. Don't overload or the chips won't cook evenly, so cook in batches if you have to.
8. Air fry at 170 degrees Fahrenheit for about 20-25 minutes, or until the chips are dry to the touch. Stir and toss the basket every 5 minutes or so, so as not to overcook.
9. Increase the temperature to 400 degrees Fahrenheit and fry for an additional 5 minutes.
10. Remove the potatoes from the air fryer and top with more vegan parmesan and salt, to taste.
11. Repeat for the other batch of potato slices. Serve and enjoy!

Tandoori Chickpeas

Servings: 4
Total Time: 30 Minutes
Ingredients and Quantity
- One 19 oz. can chickpeas (garbanzo beans), drained and rinsed
- 2 tsp. tandoori masala
- 1 tbsp. olive oil
- 3/4 tsp. salt

Direction
1. Preheat the air fryer to 375 degrees Fahrenheit.
2. In a large bowl, toss chickpeas together with the olive oil, tandoori and salt.
3. Arrange the chickpeas in a single layer in the air fryer basket and insert into the air fryer.
4. Cook for 8-10 minutes, shaking the chickpeas halfway through the cooking to ensure they cook evenly.
5. Remove the cooked chickpeas and allow to cool on a baking sheet lined with baking parchment.
6. Repeat with remaining chickpeas and serve!

Spiced Kale Chips

Servings: 3
Total Time: 25 Minutes
Ingredients and Quantity
- 3 cups or 1 large bunch kale, de-stemmed, washed and torn into biter size pieces
- 1 to 2 tbsp. za'atar seasoning
- 1 tbsp. olive oil
- 1/2 to 1 tsp. sea salt

Direction
1. Place the dried kale into a large mixing bowl, drizzle with olive oil and pour in the za'atar seasoning. Mix well to combine and coat all the kale leaves.
2. Place the kale in the air fryer basket and cook at 170 degrees Celsius.
3. The chips are ready when the edges are brown but not burnt. They should be checked on constantly during cooking to avoid burning.
4. You may also bake the kale chips at 170 degrees Celsius in an oven on a baking parchment lined baking tray.
5. They should take around 10-15 minutes. Serve and enjoy!

Garlic and Herb Chickpeas

Servings: 4
Total Time: 25 Minutes
Ingredients and Quantity
- Two 14 oz. cans chickpeas
- 1 tbsp. nutritional yeast
- 1 tbsp. olive oil
- 1 tbsp. mixed herbs (thyme, rosemary and dried oregano work well here)
- 2 tsp. garlic powder
- Sea salt and black pepper, to taste

Direction
1. Drain the chickpeas of their juice and then rinse them under a running tap.
2. Add them to a medium-sized mixing bowl and then pour in the olive oil and seasonings. Stir well, using a rubber spatula. Ensure all the chickpeas are well coated.
3. Cook the chickpeas in 2 batches, in an air fryer set at 200 degrees Celsius for 15-20 minutes. Check once at the 10-minute mark, to ensure they're cooking evenly.
4. If they pop while cooking it's totally normal as they're crisping up.
5. Once done they should be golden brown and crispy all the way through. Serve warm!
6. **Note:** Store in an air-tight container once cool, to preserve the chickpeas crispiness.

Crispy Plantain

Servings: 4
Total Time: 13 Minutes
Ingredients and Quantity
- 2 ripe plantains
- 2 tsp. natural oil (rapeseed or peanut oil work well here)
- 1/8 tsp. salt

Direction
1. Slice the plantains into 1/2 –inch thick slices at an angle,
2. In a medium bowl, toss the plantains, salt, and oil making sure that all of the pieces get well coated.
3. Transfer the plantain to the air fryer basket, and cook at 400 degrees Fahrenheit for 8-10 minutes.
4. At the 5-minute mark, shake the plantain to ensure they cook evenly.
5. The plantains are done when they're browned on the outside and moist and tender on the inside.
6. Note: Cooking times will vary depending on how ripe the plantains are. Make sure to check in at 8 minutes for doneness, and add 1 – 2 more minutes, if needed, to reach a nice, brown and crispy exterior.

Garlicky Roast Almonds

Servings: 8
Total Time: 11 Minutes
Ingredients and Quantity
- 2 cups raw almonds
- 1 tbsp. soy sauce
- 1 tsp. smoked paprika
- 1 tbsp. garlic powder
- 1/4 tsp. black pepper

Direction
1. In a large bowl, stir together paprika, garlic powder, black pepper and soy sauce, until they form a thick paste.
2. Stir in the almonds, making sure to coat all the almonds evenly.
3. Transfer the almonds to the air fryer basket, and cook at 320 degrees Fahrenheit for 6 - 8 minutes. Shake every 2 minutes to prevent sticking and burning and to ensure even cooking.
4. At the 6-minute mark, check in every minute or so, picking and tasting an almond for doneness.
5. The almonds are ready when they are slightly hard but still chewy and tender in the center. They will crunch up once cool.
6. Cool to room temperature for 10-15 minutes, and then transfer to an air tight storage container or serve. Enjoy!

Crispy Potato Peels

Servings: 1
Total Time: 16 Minutes
Ingredients and Quantity
- 2 lb. (4 medium sized potatoes) Russet potato peels
- 1/8 tsp. sea salt
- Cooking oil spray

Direction
1. Put the potato peels into the air fryer basket. Coat them with cooking oil spray and sprinkle with a pinch of salt.
2. Air fry at 400 degrees Fahrenheit for 6 - 8 minutes.
3. Halfway through cooking shake the basket and coat the peels with more cooking oil spray.
4. Towards the end of cooking, check the peels to make sure they get brown and crisp, but don't burn.
5. Serve immediately with the dip of your choice.
6. **Note:** Do not over salt the peels as they shrink when cooking so could turn out over salted. Work in batches to ensure the peels cook evenly and crisp up well, as the air fryer will not cook well if overcrowded.

Crispy Potato Chips

Servings: 4
Total Time: 20 Minutes
Ingredients and Quantity
- 400 g (or 1 large potato) Russet potato, thinly sliced
- Grape-seed cooking oil spray (you may substitute for any other, except olive oil)
- Sea salt, to taste

Direction
1. Using a kitchen paper towel, press out as much moisture as possible from the potatoes slices.
2. Spray the basket of the air fryer with the cooking oil spray and layer the potatoes, in a single layer. Work in batches to ensure even cooking.
3. Spray the tops of the potato slices with the cooking oil spray and sprinkle with sea salt.
4. Set the air fryer to 450 degrees Fahrenheit and cook for 10 – 15 minutes, until the edges of the potatoes are slightly golden brown and crisp, and the insides of the potatoes are still light in color.
5. Remove the potato chips from the air fryer and let them crisp up on the counter overnight. Enjoy!

Potato Hash

Servings: 4
Total Time: 55 Minutes
Ingredients and Quantity
- 750 g potatoes, washed, peeled or unpeeled, cut into small-sized cubes
- 250 mL egg substitute
- 3 to 5 tbsp. coconut oil, or vegan fat of your choice
- 1/2 tsp. thyme
- 1/2 tsp. savory seasoning mixture
- 1/2 tsp. black pepper
- 1/2 green pepper, washed, seeded and chopped
- 1 tsp. salt substitute
- 1 onion, medium-sized, peeled and diced

Direction
1. Preheat the air fryer to 180 C.
2. Toss the green pepper and onion with half of the coconut oil and put into the air fryer basket.
3. Toss the potatoes with the remaining coconut oil and the seasonings.
4. When the air fryer timer beeps, add the potatoes in the air fryer basket, toss the ingredients to mix and cook for 30 minutes.
5. Shake the basket after 15 minutes.
6. While the potato mixture is cooking in the air fryer, lightly grease a nonstick pan with cooking spray.
7. Grind some whole peppers into the pan and let heat for 1 minutes to develop the flavor. Add the egg substitute and cook until solid.
8. Remove from the pan, chop, and set aside.
9. When the air fryer timer beeps, add the egg to the air fryer basket and set the timer for 5 minutes.
10. Serve while piping hot with fresh tomato slices and whatever you want for breakfast. Enjoy!

Air Grilled Tomatoes

Servings: 2
Total Time: 25 Minutes
Ingredients and Quantity
- 2 tomatoes
- Your preferred herbs
- Ground black pepper, such as sage, rosemary, thyme, basil, oregano, parsley, etc.
- Cooking spray

Direction
1. Wash the tomatoes clean and then slice into halves.
2. Spray both sides of the tomatoes with 1 spray cooking spray.
3. Sprinkle the cut portion with black pepper and your choice of fresh or dried herbs.
4. With the cut side faced up, put the tomato halves in the air fryer basket.
5. Set the temperature to 160 C and the timer for 20 minutes.
6. When the timer beeps, check the doneness, and if needed, cook for a couple of minutes. Cooking time will vary on the size and ripeness of the tomatoes and your preference.
7. Serve them piping hot, at room temperature, or chilled as part of an antipasto. Enjoy!

Breakfast-Style Potatoes

Servings: 3
Total Time: 35 Minutes
Ingredients and Quantity
- 2 Russet potatoes, medium-sized, (about 13 oz. or 2 generous cups total), chopped into roughly 1 inch pieces
- 1 onion, small-sized (about 4 oz. or 3/4 cup), chopped into medium-sized pieces
- 1 bell pepper, small-sized, (about 5 oz. or 3/4 cup), chopped into medium-sized pieces
- A couple generous sprays of cooking oil spray
- Pinch salt and pepper

Direction
1. Put the potatoes in the air fryer basket.
2. Spray with cooking oil spray, shake, spray again, and sprinkle with 1 pinch salt.
3. Set the temperature to 400 F and set the timer for 10 minutes. Stop halfway during cooking to shake or stir the potatoes and continue during cooking.
4. When the ten minutes are up, add the onions and bell pepper in the air fryer.
5. Spray with cooking oil and shake the basket.
6. Cook at 400 F for another 15 minutes.
7. When there are only 5 minutes left in the cooking time, check the potatoes to ensure that they are not browning too much – cooking time will depend on the size of the potatoes.
8. Add a couple more cooking time, if needed.
9. Season with salt, to taste. Serve and enjoy!

Hot Polenta Rounds

Servings: 4
Total Time: 45 Minutes
Ingredients and Quantity
- 1 package (18 oz.) pre-cooked ancient-harvest polenta roll
- 1 tbsp. extra-virgin olive oil

Direction
1. Open the package of polenta roll.
2. Using a sharp knife, slice the polenta into 1/2-inch thick round slices.
3. Brush all the sides of the polenta slices with the olive oil.
4. Apply cooking oil onto the air fryer basket and preheat at 400 F for 5 minutes.
5. Put the polenta slices in the basket and set the timer for 25 minutes.
6. When the timer beeps, flip the slices and cook for 5-10 minutes more. Serve and enjoy!

Desserts Recipes

Buffalo Tofu

Servings: 4
Total Time: 30 Minutes
Calories: 225.3
Fat: 6.8 g
Protein: 4 g
Carbs: 41 g
Fiber: 4.8 g

Ingredients and Quantity

Dry Ingredients:
- 1/2 cup whole-wheat, gluten-free pastry flour
- 1 tbsp. ground flax seeds
- 1/4 cup cocoa powder
- 1/2 cup vegan sugar
- 1/4 tsp. salt

Wet Ingredients:
- 1/4 cup almond milk
- 1/2 tsp. pure vanilla extract
- 1/4 cup aquafaba

Extras:
- 1/4 cup hazelnuts, chopped walnuts, pecans, shredded coconut, mini vegan chocolate chips

Direction

1. Mix all the dry ingredients in one bowl.
2. In a Pyrex jug, mix all the wet and set aside.
3. Add the wet ingredients to the dry and mix to combine.
4. Add in the extra ingredients of your choice and mix again.
5. Preheat the air fryer to 350 degrees Fahrenheit.
6. Line a 5-inch cake tin with baking parchment paper if you want an oil-free recipe or spray the cake tin lightly with cooking oil spray if the recipe is not oil-free.
7. Place the pan in the air fryer basket.
8. Cook the brownies for 20 minutes. If the brownies are not done cook for 5 minutes more and repeat as needed. A cake tester inserted should come out relatively clean. Serve and enjoy!
9. **Note:** Cooking time may vary depending on the size of the cake tin and the brand of air fryer you are using.

Carrot Mug Cakes

Servings: 1
Total Time: 20 Minutes
Ingredients and Quantity

- 1/4 cups whole-wheat, gluten-free pastry flour
- 1 tbsp. brown sugar or coconut sugar
- 1/4 tsp. ground cinnamon
- 1/4 tsp. baking powder
- 2 tbsp. almond milk plus 2 tsp. more
- 1 tbsp. raisins or chopped dates
- 2 tbsp. grated carrots
- 2 tbsp. chopped walnuts
- 1/8 tsp. ground dried ginger
- A pinch allspice
- A pinch salt
- 2 tsp. flavorless oil

Direction

1. Lightly oil an oven-safe ceramic mug.
2. Add the flour, baking powder, sugar, ginger, allspice, cinnamon and salt then mix well with a fork.
3. Next add the carrot, milk, walnuts, raisins and oil and then mix again.
4. Bake in an air fryer at 350 degrees Fahrenheit for 15 minutes.
5. Check with a cake tester to make sure the middle is cooked.
6. If not, cook for 5 additional minutes.
7. Serve warm. Enjoy!

Blueberry Apple Crumble

Servings: 2
Total Time: 20 Minutes
Ingredients and Quantity

- 1 apple, finely diced
- 1/4 cup brown rice flour plus 1 tbsp. more
- 1/2 cup frozen strawberries, blueberries or peaches
- 2 tbsp. non-dairy butter
- 2 tbsp. sugar
- 1/2 tsp. ground cinnamon

Direction

1. Preheat the air fryer to 350 degrees Fahrenheit for 5 minutes.
2. Combine the apple and frozen berries or peaches in an air fryer–safe baking pan.
3. In a small bowl, combine the flour, cinnamon, sugar, and butter.
4. Spoon the crumble mixture over the fruit. Sprinkle a little extra flour all the fruit to cover any that are exposed.
5. Cook at 350 degrees Fahrenheit for 15 minutes.
6. Serve warm with dairy-free whipped cream or ice cream. Enjoy!

Apple, Strawberries and Peaches Crumble

Servings: 2
Total Time: 20 Minutes
Ingredients and Quantity
- 1 apple, finely diced
- 1/4 cup brown rice flour plus 1 tbsp. more
- 1/2 cup frozen strawberries, blueberries or peaches
- 2 tbsp. non-dairy butter
- 2 tbsp. sugar
- 1/2 tsp. ground cinnamon

Direction
1. Preheat the air fryer to 350 degrees Fahrenheit for 5 minutes.
2. Combine the apple and frozen berries or peaches in an air fryer–safe baking pan.
3. In a small bowl, combine the flour, cinnamon, sugar, and butter.
4. Spoon the crumble mixture over the fruit. Sprinkle a little extra flour all the fruit to cover any that are exposed.
5. Cook at 350 degrees Fahrenheit for 15 minutes.
6. Serve warm with dairy-free whipped cream or ice cream. Enjoy!

Cinnamon Pears

Servings: 3
Total Time: 15 Minutes
Ingredients and Quantity
- 2 unripe pears, peeled, cored, cut in half
- 2 tbsp. vegan butter
- 1 tsp. pure vanilla extract
- 1/2 tsp. cinnamon

For Garnishing:
- Sprinkle of nutmeg

Direction
1. Preheat the air fryer to 350 degrees Fahrenheit.
2. Melt the butter and add to it the vanilla extract and cinnamon, mixing well.
3. Baste the cut sides of the pears with the butter and place them cut side down into a baking pan that fits the air fryer.
4. Baste the top of the pears and bake at 350 degrees Fahrenheit for 10 minutes.
5. Flip the pears over and baste again.
6. Bake for 2 more minutes at the same temperature.
7. Give the pears a final baste and set on to serving plates.
8. Serve hot with whipped cream or ice cream. Enjoy!

Churro Doughnuts

Servings: 6
Total Time: 1 Hour 21 Minutes
Ingredients and Quantity
- 1 cup white all-purpose flour
- 1 tsp. baking powder
- 1/4 cup organic sugar
- 1/4 tsp. ground cinnamon
- 1/2 tsp. salt
- 2 tbsp. aquafaba
- 1/4 cup soy or almond milk
- 1 tbsp. coconut oil
- 2 tsp. ground cinnamon
- 2 tbsp. sugar

Direction
1. In a large bowl, combine the flour, baking powder, sugar, cinnamon and salt. Mix well to combine.
2. Add the coconut oil, aquafaba and soy milk and combine.
3. When the dough is ready, it should be a ball of slightly sticky dough.
4. Stick the dough in the refrigerator for at least 1 hour.
5. In a shallow bowl, mix together the cinnamon and the 2 tablespoons of sugar. Set this cinnamon-sugar aside.
6. Cut a piece of baking parchment paper so it covers some of the bottom of the air fryer.
7. Remove the dough from the fridge, and knead.
8. Divide into 12 pieces, forming them into balls.
9. Dredge each ball in cinnamon sugar, and put into a single layer on the baking parchment paper, leaving at least 1 inch around each ball.
10. Air fry at 370 degrees Fahrenheit for 6 minutes. Do not shake the churro balls.
11. Let the doughnuts cool for 5-10 minutes before removing from the basket.
12. Serve hot with chocolate sauce. Enjoy!

Berry Cake

Servings: 6
Total Time: 30 Minutes
Ingredients and Quantity
- 1 1/2 cup whole meal self-raising unbleaching flour
- 2/3 cup xylitol
- 3/4 cup soy milk
- 1 tsp. white vinegar
- 1 tbsp. vegetable oil
- 1 tsp. lemon zest
- 2/3 to 3/4 cup mixed berries

Direction
1. Lightly coat a 6-inch cake pan with cooking oil spray.
2. Mix the oil and xylitol in one jug and then whisk the soy milk and vinegar in a separate jug. Set aside to curdle.
3. Combine all the above mixtures and add the lemon zest, oil and berries.
4. Fold in the self-rising flour and mix well.
5. Pour the batter into the oiled cake pan and tap lightly to settle the batter.
6. Bake in the air fryer at 175 degrees Celsius for 18 – 20 minutes. Serve and enjoy!

Banana Bread

Servings: 1
Total Time: 30 Minutes
Ingredients and Quantity

- 2 small over-ripe bananas
- 2/3 cup unbleached, all-purpose flour
- 1/2 tsp. baking soda
- 1/4 tsp. sea salt
- 1/4 cup plain soy milk yogurt
- 1/3 cup sugar
- 1/4 cup walnuts
- 1/4 cup vegetable oil
- 1/2 tsp. pure vanilla extract

Direction

1. Combine the flour, baking soda and salt in a bowl.
2. In a small bowl, mix the yogurt, bananas, sugar, vegetable oil and vanilla extract.
3. Combine the wet ingredients with the dry. Don't over mix, just combine until well mixed. Fold in the walnuts at this stage.
4. Preheat the air fryer on 330 degrees Fahrenheit for 3 minutes.
5. While the air fryer is preheating, pour half the batter into one loaf pan and the other half into a second loaf pan.
6. If you have a large (6-quart) air fryer, transfer the loaf pans to the air fryer basket.
7. Air fry the banana bread at 330 degrees Fahrenheit for 20 - 22 minutes. They are done when a cake tester inserted into the loaves comes out clean.
8. Transfer the pans to a wire rack to cool for 30 minutes, before removing from the pans and serving. Enjoy!

Quinoa Carrot Cake

Servings: 6
Total Time: 12 Minutes
Ingredients and Quantity

- 1 1/2 cups cooked white quinoa
- 1/2 cup uncooked quinoa
- 1/4 cup coconut flour
- 1/2 cooked carrots puree
- 1 cup freshly grated carrots
- 3 tbsp. flaxmeal in 8 tbsp. water (allow to gel for 5 minutes)
- 1 tsp. baking soda
- 1 tsp. baking powder
- 1 tsp. cinnamon
- 1/2 tsp. nutmeg
- 1/2 tsp. ground ginger
- 2 tbsp. blackstrap molasses
- Raisins, to taste

Direction

1. Combine all the ingredients at once in a large bowl and mix well.
2. Coat a baking dish with coconut oil and pour in the cake batter.
3. Bake in the air fryer at 350 degrees Fahrenheit for 7 minutes.
4. Once done, let the cake cool and, if desired, frost with vegan cream cheese frosting. Serve and enjoy!

Semolina Cake

Servings: 6
Total Time: 60 Minutes
Ingredients and Quantity
- 1 cup fine farina, milled fine
- 2 cups hot water
- 1 cup dried fruit
- 1 cup sugar
- 1 cup almond milk
- 1/4 cup soy yogurt
- 1/4 cup coconut oil
- 1 tsp. ground cardamom'1/2 tsp. baking soda
- 1 tsp. baking powder

Direction
1. Soak the dried fruit in hot water and set aside.
2. Grease an 8-inch heat-safe baking pan and keep aside.
3. In a large mixing bowl whisk together the milk, farina, oil, sugar, soy yogurt and cardamom.
4. Set this mixture aside for 20 minutes to allow the farina to soften and absorb the liquid.
5. Drain the dried fruit well, and mix into the batter.
6. Add the baking soda and baking powder and mix well.
7. Pour the cake batter into the prepared cake pan and set the pan into the air fryer basket.
8. Set the air fryer to 330 degrees Fahrenheit for 25 minutes.
9. At the end of the bake time, insert a cake tester to check for doneness. It should come out clean.
10. Remove the pan, let rest for 10 minutes and then unmold the cake. Serve and enjoy!

Lychee Muffin

Servings: 6
Total Time: 20 Minutes
Ingredients and Quantity
- 1 1/2 cups plain flour
- 1/4 cup sugar
- 2 tsp. baking powder
- 1/2 tsp. salt

Wet Ingredients:
- 1/3 cup vegetable oil
- 1/3 cup mashed banana
- 1/3 cup soya milk

Filling:
- 1 cup lychee

Direction
1. Mix all the dry ingredients in a big bowl.
2. Stir the wet ingredients in another bowl. Just enough to roughly mix.
3. In the flour mixture (dry ingredients), form a well at the center and pour in the wet ingredients. Then fold the flour in. Give it around 14 strokes as it's okay if you still see flour bits. 4).
4. Add in the lychee and continue to fold in. It's okay for the mixture to still be wet.
5. Pre heat the air fryer to 180 degrees centigrade.
6. Into silicon cups, spoon the prepared mixture then bake in the air fryer for 10 minutes. Serve and enjoy!

Juice And Smothie Recipes

Cucumber Juice

Servings: 8
Total Time: 10 Minutes
Calories: 83.8
Fat: 0.1 g
Protein: 0.5 g
Carbs: 21.5 g
Fiber: 0.4 g
Ingredients and Quantity
- 2 peeled English cucumber
- 3/4 cup sugar
- 2 cups water
- Lime wedge, for serving

Direction
1. Add the cucumber and water to the juicer and juice.
2. Mix in the sugar.
3. Garnish with a lime wedge. Serve and enjoy!

Mellow Green Juice

Servings: 2
Total Time: 10 Minutes
Calories: 55
Fat: 1 g
Protein: 6 g
Carbs: 15 g
Fiber: 1.5 g
Ingredients and Quantity
- 1/2 bunch spinach
- 1/2 lb. celery
- 1/2 cucumber
- 12 oz. Romaine lettuce
- 1 oz. parsley
- A pinch Himalayan salt

Direction
1. Add all the fruits to the juicer and juice.
2. Mix in salt. Serve and enjoy!

Asparagus Juice

Servings: 3
Total Time: 10 Minutes
Calories: 61
Fat: 0.6 g
Protein: 3 g
Carbs: 18.6 g
Fiber: 0.9 g
Ingredients and Quantity
- 4 asparagus spears
- 3 carrots
- 2 celery stalks

Direction
1. Add all the ingredients to the juicer and juice.
2. Serve and enjoy!

Bell Pepper Juice

Servings: 1
Total Time: 10 Minutes
Calories: 63
Fat: 1 g
Protein: 4 g
Carbs: 18 g
Fiber: 0.5 g
Ingredients and Quantity
- 1 green bell pepper
- 1 red bell pepper
- 3 celery stalks
- 5 lettuce leaves
- 1/2 cucumber

Direction
1. Add all the ingredients to the juicer and juice.
2. Serve and enjoy!

Spicy Tomato Juice

Servings: 6
Total Time: 10 Minutes
Calories: 38.4
Fat: 0.2 g
Protein: 1.7 g
Carbs: 9.5 g
Fiber: 0.9 g
Ingredients and Quantity
- One 46 oz. can tomato juice (reduced sodium)
- 1/2 tsp. onion powder
- 1/2 tsp. celery seeds
- 1/2 tsp. dried basil
- 2 tbsp. wine vinegar
- 1/4 tbsp. artificial sweetener

Direction
1. Combine all the ingredients together. Mix very well.
2. Serve and enjoy!

Parsley Spinach Juice

Servings: 1
Total Time: 10 Minutes
Calories: 144.7
Fat: 1.1 g
Protein: 5 g
Carbs: 32.1 g
Fiber: 10.7 g
Ingredients and Quantity
- 6 spinach leaves
- 1 handful parsley
- 2 celery stalks
- 4 carrots, peeled

Direction
1. Add all the ingredients to the juicer and juice.
2. Serve and enjoy!

Salad Juice

Servings: 2
Total Time: 10 Minutes
Calories: 68
Fat: 0.8 g
Protein: 3.4 g
Carbs: 13.9 g
Fiber: 6.3 g

Ingredients and Quantity
- 1/2 head Romaine lettuce
- 1 medium size tomato
- 2 celery ribs
- 1 carrot
- 1 red bell pepper

Direction
1. Add all the ingredients to the juicer and juice.
2. Serve and enjoy!

Wheatgrass Juice

Servings: 2
Total Time: 10 Minutes
Calories: 74
Fat: 0.5 g
Protein: 4 g
Carbs: 18 g
Fiber: 2 g

Ingredients and Quantity
- 1 cup wheatgrass
- 1/2 lemon
- 3 carrots

Direction
1. Add all the ingredients to the juicer and juice.
2. Serve and enjoy!

Spicy Green Juice

Servings: 1
Total Time: 10 Minutes
Calories: 74
Fat: 0.5 g
Protein: 4 g
Carbs: 18 g
Fiber: 2 g

Ingredients and Quantity

- 1 cup wheatgrass
- 1/2 lemon
- 3 carrots
- 1/4 lemon
- 1 cup spinach
- 2 sprigs parsley
- 2 celery stalks
- 1/3 jalapeno pepper
- 1 tomato
- 1 pinch salt

Direction

1. Add all the ingredients to the juicer and juice.
2. Mix in salt. Serve and enjoy!

Lemony Carrot Juice

Servings: 1
Total Time: 10 Minutes
Calories: 118.6
Fat: 0.8 g
Protein: 3.6 g
Carbs: 30.9 g
Fiber: 10.6 g

Ingredients and Quantity

- 1/2 lemon
- 3 carrots
- 3 celery stalks

Direction

1. Add all the ingredients to the juicer and juice.
2. Serve and enjoy!

SECTION 3: PLANT BASED VEGANS AND VEGETARIANS AIR FRYER WEIGHT LOSS RECIPES
Air Fryer Weight Loss Recipes For Plant Based Vegans

Greek Potato Mix

Servings: 4
Total Time: 30 Minutes
Ingredients And Quantity
- 1½ pounds potatoes, peeled and cubed
- 2 tablespoons olive oil
- Salt and black pepper to taste
- 1 tablespoon hot paprika
- 2 ounces coconut cream

Direction
1. Put potatoes in a bowl and add water to cover.
2. Leave them aside for 10 minutes.
3. Drain them and mix with half of the oil, salt, pepper and the paprika and toss them.
4. Put potatoes in your air fryer's basket.
5. Cook at 360 degrees F for 20 minutes.
6. In a bowl, mix coconut cream with salt, pepper and the rest of the oil and stir well.
7. Divide potatoes between plates.
8. Add coconut cream on top. Serve and enjoy!

Tasty Mushroom Cakes

Servings: 8
Total Time: 2 Hours 18 Minutes
Ingredients And Quantity
- ounces mushrooms, chopped
- 1 small yellow onion, chopped
- Salt and black pepper to the taste
- ¼ teaspoon nutmeg, ground
- 2 tablespoons olive oil
- 1 tablespoon breadcrumbs
- 14 ounces coconut milk

Direction
1. Heat up a pan with half of the oil over medium-high heat.
2. Add onion and mushrooms.
3. Stir and cook for 3 minutes.
4. Add coconut milk, salt, pepper and nutmeg and stir.
5. Take off heat and leave aside for 2 hours.
6. In a bowl, mix the rest of the oil with breadcrumbs and stir well.
7. Take 1 tablespoon mushroom filling, roll in breadcrumbs and put them in your air fryer basket.
8. Repeat with the rest of the mushroom mix and cook cakes at 400 degrees F for 8 minutes.
9. Divide mushroom cakes between plates. Serve and enjoy!

Green Salad

Servings: 4
Total Time: 20 Minutes
Ingredients And Quantity

- 1 tablespoon lemon juice
- 4 red bell peppers
- 1 lettuce head, cut into strips
- Salt and black pepper to taste
- 3 tablespoons coconut cream
- 2 tablespoons olive oil
- 1 ounces rocket leaves

Direction

1. Place bell pepper in your air fryer's basket.
2. Cook at 400 degrees F for 10 minutes.
3. Transfer to a bowl and leave them aside to cool down.
4. Peel, cut them in strips and put them in a bowl.
5. Add rocket leaves and lettuce strips and toss.
6. In a bowl, mix oil with lemon juice, coconut cream, salt and pepper and whisk well.
7. Add over the salad, toss to coat divide between plates. Serve and enjoy!

Tomatoes Salad

Servings: 2
Total Time: 30 Minutes
Ingredients And Quantity

- 2 tomatoes, halved
- Cooking spray
- Salt and black pepper to taste
- 1 teaspoon parsley, chopped
- 1 teaspoon basil, chopped
- 1 teaspoon oregano, chopped
- 1 teaspoon rosemary, chopped
- 1 cucumber, chopped
- 1 green onion, chopped

Direction

1. Spray tomato halves with cooking oil.
2. Season with salt and pepper and place them in your air fryer's basket.
3. Cook at 320 degrees F for 20 minutes.
4. Transfer tomatoes to a bowl.
5. Add parsley, basil, oregano, rosemary, cucumber and onion,
6. Toss, serve and enjoy!

Savory French Mushroom Mix

Servings: 4
Total Time: 35 Minutes
Ingredients And Quantity

- 2 pounds mushrooms, halved
- 2 teaspoons herbs de Provence
- ½ teaspoon garlic powder
- 1 tablespoon olive oil

Direction

1. Heat up a pan with the oil over medium heat.
2. Add herbs and heat them up for 2 minutes.
3. Add mushrooms and garlic powder and stir.
4. Introduce pan in your air fryer's basket and cook at 360 degrees F for 25 minutes.
5. Divide between plates. Serve and enjoy!

Zucchini And Squash Salad

Servings: 4
Total Time: 35 Minutes
Ingredients And Quantity

- 6 teaspoons olive oil
- 1 pound zucchinis, cut into half moons
- ½ pound carrots, cubed
- 1 yellow squash, cut into chunks
- Salt and white pepper to taste
- 1 tablespoon tarragon, chopped
- 2 tablespoons tomato paste

Direction

1. In your air fryer pan, mix oil with zucchinis, carrots, squash, salt, pepper, tarragon and tomato paste.
2. Cover and cook at 400 degrees F for 25 minutes.
3. Divide between plates. Serve and enjoy!

Tasty Squash Stew

Servings: 8
Total Time: 40 Minutes
Ingredients And Quantity

- 2 carrots, chopped
- 1 yellow onion, chopped
- 2 celery stalks, chopped
- 2 green apples, cored, peeled and chopped
- 4 garlic cloves, minced
- 2 cups butternut squash, peeled and cubed
- 6 ounces canned chickpeas, drained
- 6 ounces canned black beans, drained
- 7 ounces canned coconut milk
- 2 teaspoons chili powder
- 1 teaspoon oregano, dried
- 1 tablespoon cumin, ground
- 2 cups veggie stock
- 2 tablespoons tomato paste
- Salt and black pepper to taste
- 1 tablespoon cilantro, chopped

Direction

1. In your air fryer, mix carrots with onion, celery, apples, garlic, squash, chickpeas, black beans, coconut milk, chili powder, oregano, cumin, stock, tomato paste, salt and pepper.
2. Stir, cover and cook at 370 degrees F for 30 minutes
3. Add cilantro and stir.
4. Divide into bowls and serve hot.

Chinese Green Beans Mix

Servings: 6
Total Time: 40 Minutes
Ingredients And Quantity

- 1 pound green beans, halved
- 1 cup maple syrup
- 1 cup tomato sauce
- 4 tablespoons stevia
- ¼ cup tomato paste
- ¼ cup mustard
- ¼ cup olive oil
- ¼ cup apple cider vinegar
- 2 tablespoons coconut aminos

Direction

1. In your air fryer, mix beans with maple syrup, tomato paste, stevia, tomato paste, mustard, oil, vinegar and aminos.
2. Stir, cover and cook at 365 degrees F for 35 minutes.
3. Divide into bowls and serve hot.

Black Beans Mix

Servings: 6
Total Time: 35 Minutes
Ingredients And Quantity

- 1 yellow onion, chopped
- 1 tablespoon olive oil
- 1 red bell pepper, chopped
- 1 jalapeno, chopped
- 2 garlic cloves, minced
- 1 teaspoon ginger, grated
- ½ teaspoon cumin
- ½ teaspoon allspice, ground
- ½ teaspoon oregano, dried
- 30 ounces canned black beans, drained
- ½ teaspoon stevia
- 1 cup water
- A pinch of salt and black pepper
- 3 cups brown rice, cooked
- 2 mangoes, peeled and chopped

Direction

1. In your air fryer's pan, combine onion with the oil, bell pepper, jalapeno, garlic, ginger, cumin, allspice, oregano, black beans, stevia, water, salt and pepper.
2. Stir, cover and cook at 370 degrees F for 25 minutes.
3. Add rice and mangoes
4. Toss and divide between plates. Serve and enjoy!

Okra And Eggplant Stew

Servings: 10
Total Time: 35 Minutes
Ingredients And Quantity

- 2 cups eggplant, cubed
- 1 butternut squash, peeled and cubed
- 2 cups zucchini, cubed
- 10 ounces tomato sauce
- 1 carrot, sliced
- 1 yellow onion, chopped
- ½ cup veggie stock
- 10 ounces okra
- 1/3 cup raisins
- 2 garlic cloves, minced
- ½ teaspoon turmeric powder
- ½ teaspoon cumin, ground
- ½ teaspoon red pepper flakes, crushed
- ¼ teaspoon sweet paprika
- ¼ teaspoon cinnamon powder

Direction

1.   In your air fryer, mix eggplant with squash, zucchini, tomato sauce, carrot, onion, okra, garlic, stock, raisins, turmeric, cumin, pepper flakes, paprika and cinnamon
2.   Stir, cover and cook at 360 degrees for 5 minutes.
3.   Divide into bowls. Serve and enjoy!

Savory White Beans Stew

Servings: 10
Total Time: 30 Minutes
Ingredients And Quantity

- 2 pounds white beans, cooked
- 3 celery stalks, chopped
- 2 carrots, chopped
- 1 bay leaf
- 1 yellow onion, chopped
- 3 garlic cloves, minced
- 1 teaspoon rosemary, dried
- 1 teaspoon oregano, dried
- 1 teaspoon thyme, dried
- A drizzle of olive oil
- Salt and black pepper to the taste
- 28 ounces canned tomatoes, chopped
- 6 cups chard, chopped

Direction

1.   In your air fryer's pan, mix white beans with celery, carrots, bay leaf, onion, garlic, rosemary, oregano, thyme, oil, salt, pepper, tomatoes and chard.
2.   Toss, cover and cook at 365 degrees F for 20 minutes.
3.   Divide into bowls and serve.

Spinach And Lentils Mix

Servings: 8
Total Time: 25 Minutes
Ingredients And Quantity

- 10 ounces spinach
- 2 cups canned lentils, drained
- 1 tablespoon garlic, minced
- 15 ounces canned tomatoes, chopped
- 2 cups cauliflower florets
- 1 teaspoon ginger, grated
- 1 yellow onion, chopped
- 2 tablespoons curry paste
- ½ teaspoon cumin, ground
- ½ teaspoon coriander, ground
- 2 teaspoons stevia
- A pinch of salt and black pepper
- ¼ cup cilantro, chopped
- 1 tablespoon lime juice

Direction

1. In a pan that fits your air fryer, mix spinach with lentils, garlic, tomatoes, cauliflower, ginger, onion, curry paste, cumin, coriander, stevia, salt, pepper and lime juice.
2. Stir, introduce in the air fryer and cook at 370 degrees F for 15 minutes.
3. Add cilantro and stir.
4. Divide into bowls. Serve and enjoy!

Cajun Mushrooms And Beans

Servings: 4
Total Time: 25 Minutes
Ingredients And Quantity

- 2 tablespoons olive oil
- 1 green bell pepper, chopped
- 1 yellow onion, chopped
- 2 celery stalks, chopped
- 3 garlic cloves, minced
- 15 ounces canned tomatoes, chopped
- 8 ounces white mushrooms, sliced
- 15 ounces canned kidney beans, drained
- 1 zucchini, chopped
- 1 tablespoon Cajun seasoning
- Salt and black pepper to the taste

Direction

1. In your air fryer's pan, mix oil with bell pepper, onion, celery, garlic, tomatoes, mushrooms, beans, zucchini, Cajun seasoning, salt and pepper.
2. Stir, cover and cook on at 370 degrees F for 15 minutes.
3. Divide veggie mix between plates. Serve and enjoy!

Corn And Cabbage Salad

Servings: 4
Total Time: 25 Minutes
Ingredients And Quantity

- 1 small yellow onion, chopped
- 1 tablespoon olive oil
- 2 garlic cloves, minced
- 1 and ½ cups mushrooms, sliced
- 3 teaspoons ginger, grated
- A pinch of salt and black pepper
- 2 cups corn
- 4 cups red cabbage, chopped
- 1 tablespoon nutritional yeast
- 2 teaspoons tomato paste
- 1 teaspoon coconut aminos
- 1 teaspoon sriracha sauce

Direction

1. In your air fryer's pan, mix the oil with onion, garlic, mushrooms, ginger, salt, pepper, corn, cabbage, yeast and tomato paste.
2. Stir, cover and cook at 365 degrees F for 15 minutes.
3. Add sriracha sauce and aminos, stir, divide between plates. Serve and enjoy!

Winter Green Beans

Servings: 4
Total Time: 26 Minutes
Ingredients And Quantity

- 1 small yellow onion, chopped
- 1 tablespoon olive oil
- 2 garlic cloves, minced
- 1 and ½ cups mushrooms, sliced
- 3 teaspoons ginger, grated
- A pinch of salt and black pepper
- 2 cups corn
- 4 cups red cabbage, chopped
- 1 tablespoon nutritional yeast
- 2 teaspoons tomato paste
- 1 teaspoon coconut aminos
- 1 teaspoon sriracha sauce
- 1½ cups yellow onion, chopped
- 1 pound green beans, halved
- 4 ounces canned tomatoes, chopped
- 4 garlic cloves, chopped
- 2 teaspoons oregano, dried
- 1 jalapeno, chopped
- Salt and black pepper to taste
- 1½ teaspoons cumin, ground
- 1 tablespoons olive oil

Direction

1. Preheat your air fryer to 365 degrees F.
2. Add oil to the pan, also add onion, green beans, tomatoes, garlic, oregano, jalapeno, salt, pepper and cumin.
3. Cover and cook for 16 minutes.
4. Divide between plates. Serve and enjoy!

Green Beans Casserole

Servings: 4
Total Time: 30 Minutes
Ingredients And Quantity

- 1 teaspoon olive oil
- 2 red chilies, dried
- ¼ teaspoon fenugreek seeds
- ½ teaspoon black mustard seeds
- 10 curry leaves, chopped
- ½ cup red onion, chopped
- 3 garlic cloves, minced
- 2 teaspoons coriander powder
- 2 tomatoes, chopped
- 2 cups eggplant, chopped
- ½ teaspoon turmeric powder
- ½ cup green bell pepper, chopped
- A pinch of salt and black pepper
- 1 cup green beans, trimmed and halved
- 2 teaspoons tamarind paste
- 1 tablespoons cilantro, chopped

Direction

1. In a baking dish that fits your air fryer, combine oil with chilies, fenugreek seeds, black mustard seeds, curry leaves, onion, coriander, tomatoes, eggplant, turmeric, green bell pepper, salt, pepper, green beans, tamarind paste and cilantro.
2. Toss, put in your air fryer.
3. Cook at 365 degrees F for 20 minutes.
4. Divide between plates. Serve and enjoy!

Savory Chinese Cauliflower Rice

Servings: 4
Total Time: 30 Minutes
Ingredients And Quantity

- 4 tablespoons coconut aminos
- ½ block firm tofu, cubed
- 1 cup carrot, chopped
- ½ cup yellow onion, chopped
- 1 teaspoon turmeric powder
- 3 cups cauliflower, riced
- 1½ teaspoons sesame oil
- 1 tablespoon rice vinegar
- ½ cup broccoli florets, chopped
- 1 tablespoon ginger, minced
- 2 garlic cloves, minced
- ½ cup peas

Direction

1. In a bowl, mix tofu with 2 tablespoons coconut aminos, ½ cup onion, turmeric and carrot.
2. Toss to coat and then transfer into your air fryer.
3. Cook at 370 degrees F for 10 minutes, shaking halfway.
4. In a bowl, mix cauliflower rice with the rest of the coconut aminos, sesame oil, garlic, vinegar, ginger, broccoli and peas.
5. Stir and add to the tofu mix from the fryer.
6. Toss and cook everything at 370 degrees F for 10 minutes.
7. Divide between plates. Serve and enjoy!

Tasty Artichokes Dish

Servings: 4
Total Time: 17 Minutes
Ingredients And Quantity
- 4 big artichokes
- Salt and black pepper to taste
- 2 tablespoons lemon juice
- ¼ cup olive oil
- 2 teaspoons balsamic vinegar
- 1 teaspoon oregano, dried
- 2 garlic cloves, minced

Direction
1. Season artichokes with salt and pepper.
2. Now rub them with half of the oil and half of the lemon juice.
3. Next, put them in your air fryer and cook at 360 degrees F for 7 minutes.
4. In a bowl, mix the rest of the lemon juice with vinegar, the remaining oil, salt, pepper, garlic and oregano and stir very well.
5. Divide artichokes between plates.
6. Drizzle the vinaigrette all over and serve them as side dish.

Beet Salad

Servings: 4
Total Time: 24 Minutes
Ingredients And Quantity
- 4 beets, trimmed
- 2 tablespoons balsamic vinegar
- A bunch of parsley, chopped
- Salt and black pepper to the taste
- 1 tablespoon extra-virgin olive oil
- 1 garlic clove, chopped
- 2 tablespoons capers

Direction
1. Put beets in your air fryer's basket and cook them at 360 degrees F for 14 minutes.
2. In a bowl, mix parsley with garlic, salt, pepper, olive oil and capers and stir very well.
3. Leave beets to cool down.
4. Now peel them, slice and put them in a bowl.
5. Next, add vinegar and the parsley mix.
6. Toss, divide between plates and serve as a side dish.

Creamy Brussels Sprouts

Servings: 4
Total Time: 14 Minutes
Ingredients And Quantity
- 1 pound Brussels sprouts, trimmed
- Salt and black pepper to taste
- 1 tablespoon mustard
- 2 tablespoons coconut cream
- 2 tablespoons dill, chopped

Direction
1. Put Brussels sprouts in your air fryer's basket.
2. Cook them at 350 degrees F for 10 minutes.
3. In a bowl, mix cream with mustard, dill, salt and pepper and whisk.
4. Add Brussels sprouts and toss.
5. Divide between plates and serve as a side dish.

Yellow Lentil Mix

Servings: 2
Total Time: 25 Minutes
Ingredients And Quantity

- 1 cup yellow lentils, soaked in water for 1 hour and drained
- 1 hot chili pepper, chopped
- 1-inch ginger piece, grated
- ½ teaspoon turmeric powder
- 1 teaspoon garam masala
- Salt and black pepper to taste
- 2 teaspoons olive oil
- ½ cup cilantro, chopped
- 1½ cup spinach, chopped
- 4 garlic cloves, minced
- ¾ cup red onion, chopped

Direction

1. In a pan that fits your air fryer, mix lentils with chili pepper, ginger, turmeric, garam masala, salt, pepper, olive oil, cilantro, spinach, onion and garlic.
2. Toss, introduce in your air fryer.
3. Cook at 400 degrees F for 15 minutes.
4. Divide lentil mix between plates. Serve and enjoy!

Creamy Sweet Potatoes With Zucchini

Servings: 8
Total Time: 26 Minutes
Ingredients And Quantity

- 1 cup veggie stock
- 2 tablespoons olive oil
- 2 sweet potatoes, peeled and cut into medium wedges
- 8 zucchinis, cut into medium wedges
- 2 yellow onions, chopped
- 1 cup coconut milk
- Salt and black pepper to taste
- 1 tablespoon coconut aminos
- ¼ teaspoon thyme, dried
- ¼ teaspoon rosemary, dried
- 4 tablespoons dill, chopped
- ½ teaspoon basil, chopped

Direction

1. Heat up a pan that fits your air fryer with the oil over medium heat.
2. Add onion, stir and cook for 2 minutes.
3. Add zucchinis, thyme, rosemary, basil, potato, salt, pepper, stock, milk, aminos and dill.
4. Stir and introduce in your air fryer.
5. Cook at 360 degrees F for 14 minutes.
6. Divide between plates. Serve and enjoy!

Delicious Cabbage Rolls

Servings: 8
Total Time: 35 Minutes
Ingredients And Quantity

- 2 cups cabbage, chopped
- 2 yellow onions, chopped
- 1 carrot, chopped
- ½ red bell pepper, chopped
- 1-inch piece ginger, grated
- 8 garlic cloves, minced
- Salt and black pepper to taste
- 1 teaspoon coconut aminos
- 2 tablespoons olive oil
- 10 vegan spring roll sheets
- Cooking spray
- 2 tablespoons corn flour mixed with 1 tablespoon water

Direction

1. Heat up a pan with the oil over medium-high heat.
2. Add cabbage, onions, carrots, bell pepper, ginger, garlic, salt, pepper and aminos.
3. Stir and cook for 4 minutes and then take off heat.
4. Cut each spring roll sheet and cut into 4 pieces.
5. Place 1 tablespoons veggie mix in one corner.
6. Roll and fold edges.
7. Repeat this with the rest of the rolls.
8. Place them in your air fryer's basket.
9. Grease them with cooking oil.
10. Cook at 360 degrees F for 10 minutes on each side.
11. Arrange on a platter. Serve and enjoy!

Tasty Rice Balls

Servings: 6
Total Time: 41 Minutes
Ingredients And Quantity

- 1 small yellow onion, chopped
- 1 cup Arborio rice
- 1 tablespoon olive oil
- 1 cup veggie stock
- Salt and black pepper to taste
- 2 ounces tofu, cubed
- ¼ cup sun-dried tomatoes, chopped
- 1½ cups vegan breadcrumbs
- A drizzle of olive oil
- Marinara sauce for serving

Direction

1. Heat up a pan with 1 tablespoon oil over medium heat.
2. Add onion, stir and cook for 5 minutes.
3. Add rice, stock, salt and pepper.
4. Stir and cook on a low heat for 20 minutes.
5. Now spread on a baking sheet and leave aside to cool down.
6. Transfer rice to a bowl.
7. Add tomatoes and half of the breadcrumbs and stir well.
8. Shape 12 balls and press a hole in each ball.
9. Stuff with tofu cubes and mold balls again.
10. Dredge them in the rest of the breadcrumbs.
11. Arrange all balls in your air fryer.
12. Drizzle the oil over them and cook at 380 degrees F for 10 minutes.
13. Flip them and cook for 5 minutes more.
14. Arrange them on a platter. Serve and enjoy!

Delicious Veggie Sticks

Servings: 4
Total Time: 40 Minutes
Ingredients And Quantity
- 4 parsnips, cut into thin sticks
- 2 sweet potatoes, cut into sticks
- 4 carrots, cut into sticks
- Salt and black pepper to the taste
- 2 tablespoons rosemary, chopped
- 2 tablespoons olive oil
- A pinch of garlic powder

Direction
1. Put parsnips, sweet potatoes and carrots in a bowl.
2. Now add oil, garlic powder, salt, pepper and rosemary and toss to coat.
3. Put sweet potatoes in your preheated air fryer.
4. Now cook them for 10 minutes at 350 degrees F.
5. Transfer them to a platter.
6. Add parsnips to your air fryer.
7. Cook for another 5 minutes.
8. Transfer over potato fries.
9. Add carrots and cook for another 15 minutes at 350 degrees F.
10. Transfer to the platter. Serve and enjoy!

Potato And Beans Dip

Servings: 10
Total Time: 20 Minutes
Ingredients And Quantity
- 19 ounces canned garbanzo beans, drained
- 1 cup sweet potatoes, peeled and chopped
- ¼ cup sesame paste
- 2 tablespoons lemon juice
- 1 tablespoon olive oil
- 5 garlic cloves, minced
- ½ teaspoon cumin, ground
- 2 tablespoons water
- Salt and white pepper to taste

Direction
1. Put potatoes in your air fryer's basket.
2. Now cook them at 360 degrees F for 10 minutes and cool them down.
3. Peel and put them in your food processor and then pulse well.
4. Add sesame paste, garlic, beans, lemon juice, cumin, water, oil, salt and pepper.
5. Pulse again. Then divide into bowls.
6. Serve cold and enjoy!

Fennel And Cherry Tomatoes Spread

Servings: 6
Total Time: 18 Minutes
Ingredients And Quantity
- 1 fennel bulb, cut into pieces
- 2 pints cherry tomatoes, halved
- ¼ cup veggie stock
- 5 thyme springs, chopped
- 1 tablespoons olive oil
- Salt and black pepper to taste

Direction
1. In a pan that fits your air fryer, combine fennel with tomatoes, stock, thyme, oil, salt and pepper.
2. Toss and introduce in the air fryer.
3. Cook at 365 degrees F for 12 minutes.
4. Mash the mixture with a fork.
5. Stir well and divide into bowls.
6. Serve cold and enjoy!

Easy Vegan Cinnamon Rolls

Servings: 8
Total Time: 2 Hours 15 Minutes
Ingredients And Quantity
- 1 pound vegan bread dough
- 3/4 coconut sugar
- 1½ tablespoons cinnamon powder
- 2 tablespoons vegetable oil

Direction
1. Roll dough on a floured working surface.
2. Shape to rectangle and brush with the oil.
3. In a bowl, mix cinnamon with sugar.
4. Stir and sprinkle this over dough.
5. Roll into a log.
6. Seal well and cut into 8 pieces.
7. Leave rolls to rise for 2 hours.
8. Now place them in your air fryer basket.
9. Cook at 350 degrees for 5 minutes.
10. Flip them and cook for another 4 minutes.
11. Now transfer them to a platter.
12. Serve and enjoy!

Apple Chips

Servings: 2
Total Time: 25 Minutes
Ingredients And Quantity
- 1/4 tsp. salt
- 1 tbsp. sugar
- 1/2 tsp. ground cinnamon
- 1 apple, peeled and sliced thinly

Direction
1. Preheat your Air fryer to 390 degrees F.
2. Blend the salt, sugar and cinnamon in a bowl.
3. Coat in the air fryer for 8 minutes.
4. Shake and flip halfway through the cooking time.
5. Serve and enjoy!

Crispy Tofu Bite

Servings: 4
Total Time: 1 Hour
Ingredients And Quantity
- 1 tsp. rice vinegar
- 2 tsp. toasted sesame oil
- 2 tbsp. reduced sodium soy sauce
- 1 block firm tofu, cut into cubes
- 1 tbsp. cornstarch

Direction
1. Mix the rice vinegar, sesame oil and soy sauce.
2. Soak the tofu cubes in this mixture for 30 minutes.
3. Dredge the tofu with the cornstarch.
4. Cook in the air fryer at 370 degrees F for 10 minutes.
5. Shake the air fryer and cook for another 10 minutes.

Vegan Burrito

Servings: 4
Total Time: 25 Minutes
Ingredients And Quantity
- 2 tbsp. tamari
- 3 tbsp. water, divided
- 2 tbsp. cashew butter
- 1 tbsp. liquid smoke
- 4 sheets rice paper
- ¼ cup sweet potato cubes, roasted
- 8 strips red pepper, roasted
- 1 cup broccoli florets, sautéed
- 6 stalks fresh asparagus, chopped
- 1 cup spinach, chopped

Direction
1. In a bowl, mix the tamari, 2 tablespoons water, cashew butter and liquid smoke.
2. Brush the rice papers with the remaining water.
3. Divide the vegetable fillings among the rice papers.
4. Roll them up tightly.
5. Soak each of the rolls in the mixture.
6. Place in the air fryer.
7. Cook at 350 degrees F for 10 minutes.
8. Serve and enjoy!

Taco Wraps

Servings: 4
Total Time: 35 Minutes
Ingredients And Quantity

- 1 onion, diced
- 1 red bell pepper, diced
- 2 cups corn kernels, cooked
- 4 pieces vegan fishless fillet
- ¼ cup mango salsa
- 1 cup mixed greens
- 4 tbsp. vegan cheese, shredded
- 4 large tortillas

Direction

1. In a pan over medium-low heat, sauté the onion and bell pepper for 5 minutes.
2. Add the corn and cook for 1 minute.
3. Cook the fishless fillet in the air fryer at 400 degrees F for 12 minutes.
4. Slice the fillets thinly.
5. Assemble the wraps by dividing the fishless fillets, salsa, mixed greens, onion mixture, and vegan cheese among the tortillas.
6. Wrap tightly and cook the wraps in the air fryer at 350 degrees F for 6 to 7 minutes.
7. Serve and enjoy!

Tasty Tomato Frittata

Servings: 2
Total Time: 40 Minutes
Ingredients And Quantity

- 2 tablespoons flax meal mixed with 3 tablespoons water
- ½ cup cashew cheese, shredded
- 2 tablespoons yellow onion, chopped
- Salt and black pepper to the taste
- ¼ cup coconut milk
- ¼ cup tomatoes, chopped

Direction

1. In a bowl, mix flax meal with milk, cheese, salt, pepper, onion and tomatoes.
2. Stir well and pour this into your air fryer's pan.
3. Cover and cook at 340 degrees F for 30 minutes.
4. Divide frittata between plates. Serve and enjoy!

Yam Mix

Servings: 4
Total Time: 18 Minutes
Ingredients And Quantity

- 16 ounces canned candied yams, drained
- ½ teaspoon cinnamon powder
- ¼ teaspoon allspice, ground
- ½ cup coconut sugar
- 1 tablespoon flax meal mixed with 2 tablespoons water
- 2 tablespoons coconut cream
- ½ cup maple syrup
- Cooking spray

Direction

1. In a bowl, mix yams with cinnamon and all spice.
2. Mash with a fork and stir well.
3. Grease your air fryer with cooking spray.
4. Preheat it to 400 degrees F and spread yams mix on the bottom.
5. Add sugar, flax meal, coconut cream and maple syrup and stir gently.
6. Cover and cook on for 8 minutes.
7. Divide yams mix between plates. Serve and enjoy!

Air Fryer Weight Loss Vegetarian Recipes

Spinach, Peach And Ginger Smoothie

Servings: 2
Total Time: 15 Minutes
Ingredients And Quantity
* 2 cups peaches, sliced
* 2 tsp. honey
* 1 cup baby spinach, chopped
* 1 tsp. ginger, grated
* 1¼ cups water

Direction
1. Slightly roast the peaches in the air fryer at 370 degrees F for 5 minutes and allow it to cool.
2. Put in the blender along with the rest of the ingredients.

Delicious Basil Ricotta Balls

Servings: 10
Total Time: 31 Minutes
Ingredients And Quantity
* 1 egg, yolk separated from the white
* 9 oz. ricotta, crumbled
* 2 tbsp. flour
* Salt and pepper to taste
* 1 tbsp. chives, chopped
* ½ oz. basil, chopped
* ½ cup breadcrumbs

Direction
1. In a bowl, combine the egg yolk, ricotta, flour, salt and pepper.
2. Mix well. Stir in the chives and basil.
3. Form about 20 balls from the mixture.
4. Dip the balls in the egg white.
5. Dredge with the breadcrumbs.
6. Preheat your air fryer to 390 degrees F.
7. Air fry the balls for 8 minutes per batches of 10.
8. Serve and enjoy!

Mini Mushroom Quiche Wedge

Servings: 8
Total Time: 34 Minutes
Ingredients And Quantity
* 3½ oz. ready-made pie crust
* ½ tbsp. oil
* 1 egg
* 3 tbsp. whipping cream
* 1.4 oz. cheese, grated
* Freshly ground pepper
* 4 ½ oz. mushrooms, sliced

Direction
1. Preheat your air fryer to 390 degrees F.
2. Use a cookie cutter to cut 2 small rounds from the pie crust.
3. Coat 2 small molds with oil.
4. Press the crust into the molds.
5. Place mushrooms inside the molds.
6. Beat the egg, cream and cheese.
7. Pour into the molds on top of the mushrooms.
8. Cook each mini pie in the air fryer for 12 minutes.
9. Slice into 4 wedges.
10. Serve and enjoy!

Potato-Parmesan Croquettes

Servings: 4
Total Time: 34 Minutes
Ingredients And Quantity
- 10 oz. potatoes, boiled and mashed
- 1¾ oz. Parmesan cheese, grated
- 1 egg yolk
- 2 tbsp. flour
- 1 tsp. chives, chopped
- Pinch of nutmeg
- Salt and pepper to taste
- 1 ¾ oz. breadcrumbs
- Cooking spray

Direction
1. Combine the mashed potato, cheese, egg yolk, flour and chives and mix well.
2. Season with the nutmeg, salt and pepper.
3. Preheat your air fryer to 390 degrees F.
4. Form large balls from the mixture.
5. Dredge each of the balls in the breadcrumbs.
6. Coat with the cooking spray.
7. Cook in the air fryer for 4 minutes or until it turns golden and crispy.
8. Serve and enjoy!

Tofu And Chips

Servings: 2
Total Time: 62 Minutes
Ingredients And Quantity
- ½ tbsp. lemon juice
- 7 oz. tofu, cubed
- 10 oz. potatoes, cut into strips
- Water
- 1 tbsp. vegetable oil

Direction
1. Preheat your air fryer to 360 degrees F.
2. Mix the lemon juice, salt and pepper.
3. Soak the tofu in this mixture for 5 minutes.
4. Submerge the potato strips in water for 30 minutes.
5. Cook the tofu in the air fryer for 10 minutes.
6. Next, pat the potatoes dry with a paper towel.
7. Coat with the vegetable oil.
8. Cook in the air fryer for 12 minutes, shaking 2 to 3 times while cooking.
9. Serve the tofu with the fries.

SECTION 4: VEGANS AND VEGETARIANS AIR FRYER RECIPES FOR SPECIAL SEASONS

Special seasons worth celebrating because most of them like Christmas, New Year, Easter, Independence Day, Cultural Day, Black Friday, etc. come once in a year, while some others like Thanksgiving, Holidays, Summer, etc. come at intervals.

The best way to celebrate these special seasons is to surprise your family with some special, healthy dishes. Research revealed that most people deviate from their lifestyle in the course of celebration. Most weight watchers especially consume excess calories while trying to enjoy themselves. Some others like plant based vegans and vegetarians quit their lifestyles.

That is why I have included this part in this cookbook. The main of this section is to provide you with healthy recipes that will help you maintain your lifestyle as a vegan or vegetarian while you still enjoy special occasions to the fullest.

Vegan Air Fryer Recipes For Special Seasons

Vegan Pizza

Servings: 2
Total Time: 45 Minutes
Ingredients And Quantity
- 1 vegan pizza (small)
- 1 tsp. olive oil
- 1 tbsp. pizza sauce
- 2 tbsp. caramelized onion
- 1 tbsp. vegan cheese
- 1 tbsp. basil, chopped
- 1 tbsp. black olives, sliced

Direction
1. Preheat your air fryer to 390 degrees F.
2. Brush the pizza crust with the olive oil.
3. Spread the pizza sauce on the crust.
4. Top with the onion, cheese, basil and black olives.
5. Cook for 7 minutes.
6. Serve and enjoy!

Tofu With Veggie Scramble

Servings: 3
Total Time: 50 Minutes
Ingredients And Quantity
- 2 tbsp. low sodium soy sauce
- 2 tbsp. olive oil, divided
- ½ tsp. garlic powder
- 1 tsp. turmeric
- ½ cup onion, chopped
- ½ tsp. onion powder
- 1 block tofu, cut into cubes
- 2 ½ cups potato, cubed
- 1 tbsp. olive oil
- 4 cups broccoli florets

Direction
1. Mix the soy sauce, half of the olive oil, garlic powder, turmeric, onion and onion powder in a bowl.
2. Marinate the tofu cubes in this mixture for 15 minutes.
3. Put the potatoes In another bowl and drizzle with the olive oil.
4. Air fry the potatoes at 400 degrees F for 15 minutes.
5. Shake halfway through.
6. Add the tofu and cook along with the potatoes at 370 degrees F for 10 minutes.
7. Reserve the marinade. Then toss the sweet potatoes in the remaining marinade.
8. Add these to the air fryer and cook for 5 minutes.
9. Serve and enjoy!

Tasty Buffalo Cauliflower

Servings: 4
Total Time: 20 Minutes
Ingredients And Quantity
- 1/4 cup vegan buffalo sauce
- 1/4 cup vegan butter, melted
- 4 cups cauliflower florets
- 1 cup breadcrumbs
- 1 tsp. sea salt
- Hot sauce or ranch sauce for dipping

Direction
1. Mix the buffalo sauce and butter.
2. Dip the florets into this mixture.
3. Blend the breadcrumbs and sea salt.
4. Dredge the florets with the seasoned breadcrumbs.
5. Place these in the air fryer, and cook at 350 degrees F for 15 minutes, shaking from time to time.
6. Serve with the hot sauce or ranch sauce. Enjoy!

Ranch Chickpeas

Servings: 4
Total Time: 25 Minutes
Ingredients And Quantity
- 15 oz. canned chickpeas, drained
- 2 tbsp. freshly squeezed lemon juice
- 1 tsp. sea salt
- 1 cup vegan ranch sauce

Direction
1. Toss the chickpeas in half of the olive oil.
2. Air fry the chickpeas at 400 degrees F for 15 minutes.
3. In a bowl, combine the remaining oil, lemon juice, salt and ranch sauce.
4. Coat the chickpeas in this mixture.
5. Cook in the air fryer at 350 degrees F for 5 minutes.
6. Serve and enjoy!

Asian Tofu

Servings: 4
Total Time: 1 Hour
Ingredients And Quantity
- 1 block extra firm tofu, cut into cubes
- 1 tsp. rice vinegar
- 1/4 cup soy sauce
- 1/2 tsp. garlic powder
- 1 tsp. ground ginger
- 1 tbsp. sesame oil, toasted
- ½ cup vegan mayo
- 1 tsp. sea salt
- 1 cup breadcrumbs

Direction
1. Dry the tofu by pressing with a paper towel.
2. In a bowl, combine the vinegar, soy sauce, garlic powder, ginger and sesame oil.
3. Soak the tofu cubes in this mixture.
4. Let sit for 30 minutes.
5. Put the vegan mayo in a bowl.
6. In another bowl, mix the salt and breadcrumbs.
7. Dip each cube in the mayo and then dredge with the breadcrumbs.
8. Arrange the tofu cubes in a single layer in the air fryer.
9. Cook at 370 degrees F for 20 minutes, shaking once or twice.

Baked Potato

Servings: 1
Total Time: 50 Minutes
Ingredients And Quantity

- 1 potato
- 1 tsp. olive oil
- 1/8 tsp. sea salt
- 1/4 tsp. onion powder
- 1 tsp. vegan sour cream
- 1 tbsp. chives, chopped
- 1 strip seitan bacon, cooked crisp
- 1 tbsp. Kalamata olives, sliced

Direction

1. Use a fork or knife to poke holes into the potato and rub it with oil.
2. Season with the sea salt and onion powder.
3. Cook in the air fryer at 390 degrees F for 40 minutes.
4. Turn halfway through.
5. Slice the potato and fill with the rest of the ingredients.

Crispy Fried Pickles

Servings: 7
Total Time: 25 Minutes
Ingredients And Quantity

- 1/4 dill pickles, sliced thickly
- 1/8 tsp. baking powder
- 1/8 tsp. salt
- 1/4 cup all-purpose flour
- 3 tbsp. dark German beer
- 2 tbsp. water
- 2 tbsp. cornstarch
- ¼ tsp. cayenne pepper
- ½ tsp. paprika
- 6 tbsp. panko bread crumbs
- Cooking spray
- ¼ cup vegan ranch dressing

Direction

1. Pat the pickle slices dry using a paper towel.
2. Get 3 bowls. In the first bowl, mix the baking powder, salt, flour, German beer and water.
3. Put the cornstarch in the second bowl.
4. In the third bowl, combine the cayenne pepper, paprika, and breadcrumbs.
5. Dip the pickles in each of the bowls.
6. Arrange in the air fryer.
7. Set it to 360 degrees F and cook for 8 minutes or until crispy.
8. Serve the fried pickles with the vegan ranch dressing.

Baked Potato with Chives And Spinach

Servings: 4
Total Time: 1 Hour 20 Minutes
Ingredients And Quantity

- 2 large potatoes
- 2 tsp. olive oil
- ¼ cup almond milk (unsweetened)
- ¼ cup plain vegan yogurt
- Salt and pepper to taste
- 2 tbsp. nutritional yeast
- 1 cup spinach, chopped
- 1 tbsp. chives, chopped

Direction

1. Rub the potatoes with the olive oil.
2. Set your air fryer to 390 degrees F.
3. Cook the potatoes in the air fryer for 30 minutes.
4. Flip the potatoes and cook for another 30 minutes.
5. Slice the potatoes in half and scoop out some of the flesh.
6. Mash the flesh and mix with the almond milk, yogurt, salt, pepper and nutritional yeast.
7. Put the mixture back into the potato shells.
8. Top with the spinach and chives.
9. Cook in the air fryer for 5 minutes more.
10. Serve while warm.

Delicious Spinach And Tempeh Balls

Servings: 6
Total Time: 25 Minutes
Ingredients And Quantity

- 1 cup spinach, chopped
- 1 cup tempeh, grated
- 1/4 cup breadcrumbs
- 1 tsp. garlic, grated
- 1 onion, chopped
- ¼ cup corn flour
- Salt to taste
- 1 tsp. oil

Direction

1. Put the spinach leaves in a food processor.
2. Pulse until smooth.
3. Blend the spinach paste with the tempeh, breadcrumbs, garlic, onion, corn flour and a little salt.
4. Form into balls and brush with olive oil.
5. Set air fryer to 200 degrees F.
6. Cook for 15 minutes.

Tasty Veggie Rolls

Servings: 2
Total Time: 35 Minutes
Ingredients And Quantity
- 2 cups flour
- 1 tsp. baking powder
- Pinch of salt
- Pinch of oregano
- ¼ cup almond milk
- 1 tsp. olive oil
- 1 tbsp. onion, chopped
- ¼ cup potato, chopped
- ¼ cup carrot, grated
- ½ cup beans, sliced
- 2 tsp. cornstarch
- 2 tsp. corn flour

Direction
1. Combine the flour, baking powder, salt, oregano and milk.
2. Knead until you form a dough.
3. Heat the oil in a pan.
4. Sauté the onion until soft.
5. Add the rest of the vegetables.
6. Cook until the vegetables are tender.
7. Create a round shape wrapper using the dough you made earlier.
8. Roll to flatten. Add the vegetables and wrap tightly.
9. Dust with the corn flour and cornstarch.
10. Air fry at 200 degrees F for 15 minutes.

Paprika Tofu

Servings: 2
Total Time: 17 Minutes
Ingredients And Quantity
- 1 block extra firm tofu
- 1 tbsp. smoked paprika
- 1/4 cup cornstarch
- Salt and pepper to taste

Direction
1. Press the tofu with a paper towel to get the moisture out, then cut into bite size pieces.
2. Combine the paprika and cornstarch.
3. Sprinkle this mixture onto the tofu cubes.
4. Season the tofu with the salt and pepper.
5. Cook in the air fryer at 370 degrees F for 12 minutes.
6. Shake every 4 minutes to cook evenly.

Bacon Cashews

Servings: 4
Total Time: 15 Minutes
Ingredients And Quantity
- 3 tbsp. liquid smoke
- 2 tsp. salt
- 3 cups raw cashews
- 2 tbsp. blackstrap molasses

Direction
1. Combine all the ingredients in a bowl.
2. Place the cashews in the air fryer.
3. Set the air fryer to 350 degrees F.
4. Cook the cashews for 10 minutes.
5. Shake every 2 to 3 minutes.
6. Allow to cool before you serve.

Black Beans With Guacamole And Sweet Potato

Servings: 6
Total Time: 28 Minutes
Ingredients And Quantity
- 2 sweet potatoes, roasted
- 2 tbsp. soy milk
- 15 oz. canned black beans, rinsed and drained
- Salt and papper to taste
- 1 cup vegan cheese, shredded
- ½ tsp. cumin
- ½ tsp. garlic powder
- ¾ tsp. onion powder
- 12 small corn tortillas
- Cooking spray
- 1 cup guacamole

Direction
1. Mash the sweet potatoes in a bowl and add the soy milk.
2. Add the black beans, salt, pepper, vegan cheese, cumin, garlic powder and onion powder.
3. Top each of the tortillas with this filling.
4. Roll up the tortillas.
5. Coat air fryer basket with cooking spray.
6. Place the tortillas inside.
7. Cook at 390 degrees F for 8 minutes.
8. Serve with the guacamole.

Spring Rolls

Servings: 4
Total Time: 25 Minutes
Ingredients And Quantity

- 1 oz. mushrooms, sliced
- 1 oz. carrot, cut into strips
- 1 stalk celery, chopped
- 1 tsp. sugar
- ½ tsp. ginger, grated
- Salt to taste
- 1 vegan egg replacer
- 1 tsp. cornstarch
- 8 spring roll wrappers

Direction

1. Mix the mushroom, carrot and celery.
2. Add the sugar, ginger and salt.
3. In another bowl, combine the vegan egg and cornstarch.
4. Put the mushroom mixture on top of each spring roll wrapper.
5. Roll it up and seal the edges by brushing with the vegan egg mixture.
6. Preheat the air fryer to 390 degrees F.
7. Cook for 4 minutes or until golden brown.

Tasty Mapple Chickpeas

Servings: 4
Total Time: 18 Minutes
Ingredients And Quantity

- 15 oz. canned chickpeas
- 1 tbsp. maple syrup
- 2 tbsp. aquafaba from chickpeas
- 1/2 tsp. salt
- 2 tsp. smoked paprika
- 1 ½ tsp. garlic powder

Direction

1. Drain the chickpeas but reserve the liquid.
2. Add the chickpeas to the air fryer.
3. Cook at 390 degrees F for 8 minutes.
4. In a bowl, mix the maple syrup, aquafaba, salt, paprika and garlic powder.
5. Add the chickpeas to the mixture.
6. Put the chickpeas back in the air fryer.
7. Cook at 390 degrees F for 5 minutes.

Roasted Cauliflower Florets

Servings: 2
Total Time: 45 Minutes
Ingredients And Quantity

- 1 medium cauliflower, cut into florets
- 1 tbsp. olive oil
- Salt and pepper to taste
- 1 tbsp. vegan butter
- 2 tbsp. onion, chopped
- 2 tbsp. whisky
- ¼ tsp. stock vegetable cube
- ¼ cup water
- ¼ cup low fat vegan cream
- 2 cups salad greens
- ¼ cup cherry tomatoes, sliced

Direction

1. Coat the cauliflower florets with the oil.
2. Season with the salt and pepper.
3. Cook in the air fryer at 390 degrees F for 6 to 8 minutes.
4. Prepare the sauce by melting the butter in a pan over medium heat.
5. Sauté the onion for 5 minutes.
6. Turn off the heat and add the whisky.
7. Once the whisky sizzles, start the flame.
8. Simmer for 4 minutes.
9. Add the stock cube and simmer for another 4 minutes.
10. Add the cream and simmer for 5 minutes more.
11. Season with the salt and pepper.
12. Serve with the salad greens and cherry tomatoes topped with the vegan cream.

Vegetarian Air Fryer Recipes For Special Seasons

Basil And Broccoli Pizza

Servings: 4
Total Time: 47 Minutes
Ingredients And Quantity

- 1 sachet instant yeast
- 17 0z. flour
- 2 tbsp. olive oil
- 250 ml. water
- 100 ml tomato sauce
- 100 ml cream
- 1 oz. fresh basil, chopped
- 14 oz. broccoli florets, boiled and chopped
- 3 spring onions, sliced
- Salt and pepper to taste
- 5 oz. cheddar cheese

Direction

1. Put the yeast, flour, olive oil and water in a food processor.
2. Now pulse until well blended.
3. Knead the dough on a floured working surface.
4. Form a ball and wrap it in cling.
5. Chill the dough in the refrigerator for 30 minutes.
6. Take the dough out of the refrigerator.
7. Preheat the air fryer to 390 degrees F.
8. Roll the dough and flatten with rolling pin.
9. Spread a layer of the tomato sauce, and then the cream.
10. Top with the basil, broccoli and spring onions.
11. Season with the salt and pepper.
12. Put a layer of cheese on top.
13. Cook for 7 minutes in the air fryer.
14. Serve and enjoy!

Roasted Potatoes With Spicy Paprika

Servings: 4
Total Time: 1 Hour
Ingredients And Quantity

- 28 oz. potatoes, peeled and cubed
- Salt and pepper to taste
- 1 tbsp. spicy paprika
- 2 tbsp. olive oil, divided
- 2 cups Greek yogurt

Direction

1. Preheat your air fryer to 360 degrees F.
2. Soak the potatoes in water for half an hour.
3. Drain and pat dry using paper towel.
4. In a bowl, mix the salt, pepper, paprika and half of the oil.
5. Coat the potatoes in this mixture.
6. Cook in the air fryer for 20 minutes, shaking once in a while.
7. While waiting, blend the remaining oil and yogurt.
8. Season with the salt and pepper.
9. Serve the potatoes with the yogurt mixture as the dipping sauce. Enjoy!

Green Salad With Yogurt And Roasted Pepper

Servings: 4
Total Time: 15 Minutes
Ingredients And Quantity

- 1 red bell pepper, cut into strips
- 2 tbsp. olive oil
- 1 tbsp. freshly squeezed lemon juice
- 3 tbsp. yogurt
- Salt and pepper to taste
- 2 cups rocket leaves, chopped
- 4 cups Romaine lettuce, cut into strips

Direction

1. Preheat your air fryer to 390 degrees F.
2. Roast the bell pepper strips for 10 minutes.
3. In a bowl, mix the oil, lemon juice and yogurt.
4. Season with the salt and pepper.
5. Toss the rocket leaves and Romaine lettuce in this dressing.
6. Top with the bell pepper strips.
7. Serve and enjoy!

Mushroom Croquettes

Servings: 8
Total Time: 2 Hours 23 Minutes
Ingredients And Quantity

- ¼ onion, chopped
- ½ cup mushrooms, chopped
- 1 tbsp. butter
- 1½ tbsp. flour
- 500 ml milk
- Salt and nutmeg to taste
- 2 tbsp. vegetable oil
- 1 ¾ oz. breadcrumbs

Direction

1. Sauté the onion and mushrooms in the butter.
2. Add the flour and mix well.
3. Add the milk and blend.
4. Season with the salt and nutmeg.
5. Remove from heat and let cool.
6. Chill in the refrigerator for 2 hours.
7. Meanwhile, combine the oil and breadcrumbs.
8. Take out the mushroom mixture from the refrigerator.
9. Form large balls from the breadcrumbs.
10. Roll into the breadcrumbs.
11. Cook in the air fryer at 390 degrees F for 8 mi nutes or until it turns golden brown.
12. Serve and enjoy!

Tasty Thai Mango Cakes

Servings: 4
Total Time: 22 Minutes
Ingredients And Quantity
- 1 ½ tsp. red chili paste, divided
- 1 ripe mango, cubed
- 3 tbsp. parsley, chopped and divided
- 1 tbsp. lime juice, divided
- 1 tsp. lime zest, divided
- 1 green onion, chopped
- 4 tbsp. ground coconut

Direction
1. In a food processor, combine ½ teaspoon of chili paste, the mango, 1 tablespoon of the parsley, half of the lime juice and half of the lime zest.
2. Now pulse until smooth.
3. Add the rest of the parsley, along with the green onion and 2 tablespoons ground coconut.
4. Place the remaining coconut on a plate.
5. Form round shapes from the mixture and coat with the ground coconut.
6. Cook in the air fryer at 370 degrees for 7 minutes or until golden brown.

Crispy Vegetarian Spring Rolls

Servings: 4
Total Time: 24 Minutes
Ingredients And Quantity
- 1 oz. mushrooms, chopped
- 4 oz. tofu, cubed and fried
- 1 oz. carrot, sliced thinly
- 1 stalk celery, chopped
- 1 tsp. sugar
- ½ tsp. ginger, chopped
- 1 tsp. vegetable stock powder
- 1 egg
- 1 tsp. cornstarch
- 8 spring roll wrappers
- Cooking spray

Direction
1. Combine the mushrooms, tofu, carrots and celery in a bowl.
2. Add the sugar, ginger and vegetable stock powder and then mix well.
3. In another bowl, beat the egg and mix in the cornstarch.
4. Put the mushroom mixture on top of each roll wrapper.
5. Roll it up and brush the edges with the egg mixture to seal.
6. Coat the rolls with cooking spray.
7. Cook in the air fryer at 390 degrees F for 4 minutes.

Roasted Winter Veggies

Servings: 6
Total Time: 40 Minutes
Ingredients And Quantity

- 10 oz. butternut squash, cut into cubes
- 10 oz. celery root, cut into cubes
- 10 oz. parsnip, cut into cubes
- 2 onions, cut into wedges
- 1 tbsp. olive oil
- 1 tbsp. thyme, chopped
- Salt and pepper to taste

Direction

1. Preheat your air fryer to 390 degrees F.
2. Coat all the vegetables in olive oil.
3. Season with the thyme, salt and pepper.
4. Cook in the air fryer for 20 minutes.
5. Shake once or twice when roasting it.
6. Serve and enjoy!

Vegetarian Burger With Boiled Potatoes

Servings: 4
Total Time: 23 Minutes
Ingredients And Quantity

- 14 oz. veggie meat, minced
- 1 onion, chopped
- ½ cup carrot, grated
- 1 green onion grated
- 1 green onion chopped
- 1 egg
- Salt and pepper to taste
- Pinch of nutmeg
- 3 tbsp. breadcrumbs
- 2 cups boiled potato cubes

Direction

1. Preheat your air fryer to 390 degree F.
2. Combine all the ingredients and mix well.
3. From burger patties from the mixture.
4. Cook for about 8 minutes.
5. Serve with the boiled potatoes.

Pizza With Arugula And Mushrooms

Servings: 1
Total Time: 27 Minutes
Ingredients And Quantity

- 1 tsp. instant yeast
- 3½ oz. flour
- 1/8 tsp. salt
- ½ tbsp. olive oil
- 60 ml water
- 50 ml tomato sauce
- ½ cup mozzarella cheese, shredded
- 5 mushrooms, sliced in half
- 1 cup arugula, chopped
- Black pepper to taste
- 2 tsp. dried oregano
- 1 tbsp. Parmesan cheese, grated

Direction

1. In a bowl, combine the yeast, flour, salt and oil.
2. Mix well while gradually adding the water.
3. Knead the dough well until it becomes elastic.
4. Preheat your air fryer to 390 degrees F.
5. Coat a small cooking pan with the cooking spray.
6. Press the dough into the pan.
7. Spread a layer of the tomato sauce on the pizza dough.
8. Sprinkle the mozzarella on top.
9. Arrange the mushrooms and arugula.
10. Season with the pepper, oregano and arugula.
11. Bake in the air fryer for 12 minutes.
12. Serve and enjoy!

SECTION 5: 40 DAYS AIR FRYER MEAL PREP RECIPES FOR VEGANS AND VEGETARIANS
Meal Prep Diet Tips

Meal Prep is simply the act of preparing your meals ahead of time so that every day you know exactly what to eat and it is ready for you. All you need to do is to take it out of your storage container (like refrigerator, deep freezer), heat it up and eat. This act takes the guesswork and impulse out of your diet. All you need to do is to sit down once in a week and arrange things you will eat throughout a week (this is called meal planning phase) and then prepare and store them ahead of time.

This saves you the stress of having to cook every single day. You now cook once in a week and still eat healthy meals. This act also goes a long way to help you meet up with your weight loss goal.

Some Meal Prep Success Tips

Here are some tips that will help you in your meal prep lifestyle
1.   **Learn to Store up in a Container**In order to pack a week's worth of meals, you are going to need a week's worth of containers. The easiest way to go about this to buy a set or two matching boxes which will make packing of prepared meals in the fridge easier for you. The containers must not match, you can also use mismatching containers. You will need smaller containers for storing salad dressings or dip.
2.   **Learn to Repeat Some Meals**In order to save time, repeat a few lunch components within a week. But space the repetition out throughout the week. For instance, your Tuesday's turkey wrap can also be packed for Friday's salad dip, etc.
3.   **Freeze up Things**Freezing is one of the best ways to store up food items without tampering with their nutritional values. For instance, freezing yogurt prevents them from sloshing about in the lunch box. The same applies to some other food items like apple sauce, corn peas, cooked edamame, etc.
4.   **Try to Figure Out Recipes that Can Last**It requires some trial and error to understanding what recipes are worthy of packing for a week's worth of launches. This study will also help you know how to fix those food stuffs that cannot last up to a week earlier in your week's food menu. (This is called strategic planning). For instance, sliced strawberries will be mushy by mid-week. So the best option is to fix them up in the Monday or Tuesday launch box.

30 Days Meal Prep Diet Plan For Vegans

Day 1: Tasty Pear Oatmeal

Servings: 2
Total Time: 25 Minutes
Ingredients And Quantity
*   2 cups coconut milk
*   ½ cup steel cut oats
*   ½ teaspoon vanilla extract
*   1 pear, chopped
*   ½ teaspoon maple extract
*   1 tablespoon stevia

Direction
1.   In your air fryer pan, mix coconut milk with oats, vanilla, pear, maple extract and stevia.
2.   Stir, cover and cook at 360 degrees F for 15 minutes.
3.   Divide into bowls. Serve and enjoy!

Day 2: Apple Steel Cut Oats

Servings: 6
Total Time: 25 Minutes
Ingredients And Quantity

- 1½ cups water
- 1½ cups coconut milk
- ¼ teaspoon allspice, ground
- ¼ teaspoon ginger powder
- 2 apples, cored, peeled and chopped
- 1 cup steel cut oats
- ½ teaspoon cinnamon powder
- ¼ teaspoon nutmeg, ground
- ¼ teaspoon cardamom, ground
- 1 tablespoon flaxseed, ground
- 2 teaspoons vanilla extract
- 2 teaspoons stevia
- Cooking spray

Direction

1. Spray your air fryer with cooking spray, add apples, milk, water, cinnamon, oats, allspice, nutmeg, cardamom, ginger, vanilla, flaxseeds and stevia.
2. Stir, cover and cook at 360 degrees F for 15 minutes.
3. Divide into bowls. Serve and enjoy!

Day 3: Blueberries Oats

Servings: 6
Total Time: 25 Minutes
Ingredients And Quantity

- 1 cup blueberries
- 1 cup steel cut oats
- 1 cup coconut milk
- 2 tablespoons agave nectar
- ½ teaspoon vanilla extract
- Cooking spray

Direction

1. Spray your air fryer with cooking spray, add oats, milk, agave nectar, vanilla and blueberries.
2. Toss, cover and cook at 365 degrees F for 10 minutes.
3. Divide into bowls.
4. Serve and enjoy!

Day 4: Banana And Walnuts Oats

Servings: 4
Total Time: 25 Minutes
Ingredients And Quantity

- 1 banana, peeled and mashed
- 1 cup steel cut oats
- 2 cups almond milk
- 2 cups water
- ¼ cup walnuts, chopped
- 2 tablespoons flaxseed meal
- 2 teaspoons cinnamon powder
- 1 teaspoon vanilla extract
- ½ teaspoon nutmeg, ground

Direction

1. In your air fryer mix oats with almond milk, water, walnuts, flaxseed meal, meal, cinnamon, vanilla and nutmeg.
2. Stir, cover and cook at 360 degrees F for 15 minutes.
3. Divide into bowls. Serve and enjoy!

Day 5: Cranberry Coconut Quinoa

Servings: 4
Total Time: 23 Minutes
Ingredients And Quantity

- 1 cup quinoa
- 3 cups coconut water
- 1 teaspoon vanilla extract
- 3 teaspoons stevia
- 1/8 cup coconut flakes
- ¼ cup cranberries, dried
- 1/8 cup almonds, chopped

Direction
1. In your air fryer, mix quinoa with coconut water, vanilla, stevia, coconut flakes, almonds and cranberries.
2. Toss, cover and cook at 365 degrees F for 13 minutes.
3. Divide into bowls. Serve and enjoy!

Day 6: Mediterranean Chickpeas

Servings: 2
Total Time: 22 Minutes
Ingredients And Quantity

- Cooking spray
- 3 shallots, chopped
- 2 garlic cloves, minced
- ½ teaspoon sweet paprika
- ½ teaspoon smoked paprika
- ½ teaspoon cinnamon powder
- Salt and black pepper to the taste
- 2 tomatoes, chopped
- 2 cup chickpeas, cooked
- 1 tablespoon parsley, chopped

Direction
1. Spray your air fryer with cooking spray and preheat it to 365 degrees F.
2. Add shallots, garlic, sweet and smoked paprika, cinnamon, salt, pepper, tomatoes, parsley and chickpeas.
3. Toss, cover and cook for 12 minutes.
4. Divide into bowls. Serve and enjoy!

Day 7: Pumpkin Muffins

Servings: 2
Total Time: 20 Minutes
Ingredients And Quantity

- 1½ cups rolled oats
- ½ cup pumpkin, peeled and cubed
- ¼ cup maple syrup
- 1 teaspoon cinnamon powder
- ¼ teaspoon nutmeg, ground
- ¼ teaspoon ginger powder
- 1/3 cup cranberries

Direction
1. In your blender, mix oats with pumpkin, maple syrup, cinnamon, ginger and nutmeg and pulse well.
2. Fold cranberries into the mix, spoon the whole mix into muffin cups.
3. Place them in your air fryer's basket, cover and cook at 360 degrees F for 10 minutes.
4. Serve and enjoy!

Day 8: Broccoli And Tofu Bowls

Servings: 2
Total Time: 25 Minutes
Ingredients And Quantity

- 1 block firm tofu, pressed and cubed
- 1 teaspoon rice vinegar
- 2 tablespoons coconut aminos
- 1 tablespoon olive oil
- 1 cup quinoa, cooked
- 4 cups broccoli florets
- 2 tablespoons vegan avocado pesto

Direction

1. In a bowl, mix tofu cubes with vinegar, coconut aminos, oil and broccoli.
2. Toss and leave aside for 10 minutes.
3. Transfer tofu to your air fryer's basket and cook at 400 degrees F for 10 minutes.
4. Add broccoli, cover fryer again and cook for 5 minutes more.
5. Divide quinoa into bowls.
6. Add tofu and broccoli.
7. Top with avocado pesto. Serve and enjoy!

Day 9: Coconut Rice

Servings: 4
Total Time: 25 Minutes
Ingredients And Quantity

- 1 cup Arborio rice
- 2 cups almond milk
- 1 cup coconut milk
- 1/3 cup agave nectar
- 2 teaspoons vanilla extract
- ¼ cup coconut flakes, toasted

Direction

1. In your air fryer, mix rice with almond milk, coconut milk, agave nectar, vanilla extract and coconut flakes.
2. Cover and cook at 360 degrees F for 15 minutes.
3. Divide into bowls. Serve warm.

Day 10: Eggplant Sandwich

Servings: 2
Total Time: 60 Minutes
Ingredients And Quantity

- 1 eggplant, sliced
- 2 teaspoons parsley, dried
- Salt and black pepper to taste
- ½ cup vegan breadcrumbs
- ½ teaspoon Italian seasoning
- ½ teaspoon garlic powder
- ½ teaspoon onion powder
- 2 tablespoons almond milk
- 4 vegan bread slices
- Cooking spray
- ½ cup avocado mayo
- ¾ cup tomato sauce
- A handful basil, chopped

Direction

1. Season eggplant slices with salt and pepper.
2. Leave aside for 30 minutes and then pat dry them well.
3. In a bowl, mix parsley with breadcrumbs, Italian seasoning, onion and garlic powder, salt and black pepper and stir.
4. In another bowl, mix milk with vegan mayo and also stir well.
5. Brush eggplant slices with mayo mix.
6. Dip them in breadcrumbs mix.
7. Place them on a lined baking sheet and spray with cooking oil.
8. Introduce baking sheet in your air fryer's basket and cook them at 400 degrees F for 15 minutes, flipping them halfway.
9. Brush each bread slice with olive oil and arrange 2 of them on a working surface.
10. Add baked eggplants slices.
11. Spread tomato sauce and basil and top with the other bread slices, greased side down.
12. Divide between plates. Serve and enjoy!

Day 11: Coffee Donuts With Maple Cashew Cream

Servings: 6
Total Time: 1 Hour 21 Minutes
Ingredients And Quantity

- 1 tsp. baking powder
- 1 cup all-purpose flour
- 1/2 tsp. salt
- 1/4 cup sugar
- 1 tbsp. sunflower oil
- 2 tbsp. aquafaba from white beans
- 1 tsp. coffee extract
- ¼ cup coffee
- ½ cup raw cashews, soaked in boiling water for 20 minutes
- 1½ tbsp. maple syrup

Direction

1. Mix the baking powder, flour, salt and sugar in a bowl.
2. Add the oil, aquafaba, coffee extract and coffee. Then mix well.
3. Chill the dough in the refrigerator for 1 hour.
4. While waiting, make the maple-cashew cream.
5. Drain the cashews and puree in a blender with the maple syrup until smooth.
6. Take the dough from the refrigerator.
7. Put a parchment paper at the bottom of the air fryer but leave a little space on the sides for air circulation.
8. Form 12 donuts from the dough.
9. Place these in the air fryer in batches.
10. Cook at 370 degrees F for 6 minutes but do not shake.
11. Allow to cool before you serve and serve with maple cashew cream.

Day 12: Roasted Figs, Salad And Chickpeas

Servings: 2
Total Time: 22 Minutes
Ingredients And Quantity
- 8 figs, stemmed and cut in half
- 3 tbsp. balsamic vinegar, divided
- 2 tbsp. olive oil
- Salt and pepper to taste
- 1 tsp. oil
- 1 tsp. cumin seeds, roasted and crushed
- 1 ½ cups chickpeas, cooked
- 3 cups arugula rocket, chopped

Direction
1. Toss the figs in 1 tablespoon of the balsamic vinegar.
2. Roast in the air fryer at 390 degrees F for 7 minutes.
3. Get the juice from the roasted figs and put it in a bowl.
4. Add the olive oil, remaining vinegar, salt and pepper. Then mix well.
5. In a pan, pour the oil and add the cumin, salt and chickpeas.
6. Cook for 3 to 5 minutes.
7. Serve the arugula with the figs and chickpeas.

Day 13: Veggie Pancake

Servings: 8
Total Time: 15 Minutes
Ingredients And Quantity
- 1/2 tsp. baking powder
- 1/2 cup whole wheat flour
- 1/2 tsp. salt
- 1/4 tsp. pepper
- ¼ cup almond milk
- 1 cup carrots, grated
- 1 cup zucchini, grated
- 2 green onions, sliced
- Cooking spray

Direction
1. Put the baking powder, flour, salt and pepper in a bowl.
2. In another bowl, mix the vegetables and milk.
3. Add this mixture to the first bowl. Mix well.
4. Coat the air fryer basket with cooking spray.
5. Cook the pancakes in batches at 370 degrees F for 2 to 3 minutes or until golden.
6. Flip to cook the other side for 2 minutes.

Day 14: Beet Salad With Avocado

Servings: 4
Total Time: 17 Minutes
Ingredients And Quantity
- 8 oz. beets, chopped
- Cooking spray
- 5 oz. kale, chopped
- 2 avocados, sliced
- 4 Portobello mushroom caps
- 3 tbsp. olive oil
- ¼ cup lemon juice
- 1 shallot, chopped

Direction
1. Coat the beets with cooking spray.
2. Cook in the air fryer at 390 degrees F for 7 minutes.
3. Put the beets in a salad bowl.
4. Add the kale, avocados and mushrooms.
5. In another bowl, mix the olive oil, lemon juice and shallots.

Day 15: Delicious Butternut Squash And Rice Bowl

Servings: 2
Total Time: 27 Minutes
Ingredients And Quantity
- 2 cups butternut squash cubes
- 1/2 onion, cut into wedges
- Cooking spray
- 1/2 tsp. vegetable stock powder
- Salt and pepper to taste
- ½ tsp. dried oregano
- ½ cup coconut milk
- ¾ cup vegetable stock
- 1 cup cooked rice
- ¼ cup cilantro
- ½ cup parsley, chopped

Direction
1. Coat the squash and onions with cooking spray.
2. Season with the vegetable stock powder, salt, pepper and oregano. Cook in the air fryer at 370 degrees F
3. Cook in the air fryer at 370 degrees F for10 minutes.
4. Shake several times to cook evenly.
5. In a skillet over medium heat, warm the coconut milk and vegetable stock.
6. Add the roasted squash and onions.
7. Simmer for 7 minutes.
8. In a bowl, place the cooked rice and top with the squash mixture.
9. Garnish with the cilantro and parsley before serving. Enjoy!

Day 16: Tasty Kale Sandwich

Servings: 1
Total Time: 16 Minutes
Ingredients And Quantity
- A drizzle of olive oil
- 2 cups kale, torn
- A pinch of salt and black pepper
- 2 tablespoons pumpkin seeds
- 1 small shallot, chopped
- ½ teaspoon jalapeno, dried and crushed
- 1½ tablespoons avocado mayonnaise
- 1 avocado slice
- 1 vegan bun, halved

Direction
1. Heat up your air fryer with the oil at 360 degrees F
2. Now add kale, salt, pepper, pumpkin seeds, shallot and jalapeno, toss and cover it.
3. Cook for 6 minutes shaking once.
4. Spread avocado mayo on each muffin half.
5. Add the avocado slice.
6. Add the kale mix.
7. Top with the muffin half.
8. Serve and enjoy!

Day 17: Savory Vegan Frittata

Servings: 3
Total Time: 20 Minutes
Ingredients And Quantity
- ½ vegan sausage, sliced
- 2 tablespoons flax meal mixed with 3 tablespoons water
- 4 cherry tomatoes, halved
- 1 tablespoon parsley, chopped
- 1 tablespoon olive oil
- Salt and black pepper to the taste

Direction
1. Put oil, tomatoes and vegan sausage in your air fryer's pan.
2. Preheat at 360 degrees F and bake for 5 minutes.
3. Add flax meal, parsley, salt and pepper, toss, spread in the pan, cover and cook at 360 degrees F for 5 minutes more.
4. Slice, divide between plates. Serve and enjoy!

Day 18: Scrambled Tofu

Servings: 4
Total Time: 40 Minutes
Ingredients And Quantity

- 2 tablespoons coconut aminos
- 1 block firm tofu, cubed
- 1 teaspoon turmeric powder
- 2 tablespoons olive oil
- ½ teaspoon onion powder
- ½ teaspoon garlic powder
- 2½ cup red potatoes, cubed
- ½ cup yellow onion, chopped
- Salt and black pepper to the taste

Direction

1. In a bowl, mix tofu with 1 tablespoon oil, salt, pepper, coconut aminos, garlic and onion powder, turmeric and onion and toss to coat.
2. In another bowl, mix potatoes with the rest of the oil, salt and pepper and toss.
3. Put potatoes in preheated air fryer at 350 degrees F and bake for 15 minutes, shaking them halfway.
4. Add tofu and the marinade and bake at 350 degrees F for 15 minutes.
5. Divide between plates. Serve and enjoy!

Day 19: Beans Burrito

Servings: 2
Total Time: 20 Minutes
Ingredients And Quantity

- 2 cups baked black beans
- Cooking spray
- ½ red bell pepper, sliced
- 1 small avocado, peeled, pitted and sliced
- 2 tablespoons vegan salsa
- Salt and black pepper to the taste
- 1/8 cup cashew cheese, grated
- Vegan tortillas for serving

Direction

1. Grease your air fryer with the cooking spray.
2. Now add black beans, bell pepper, salsa, salt and pepper.
3. Cover and cook at 400 degrees F for 6 minutes.
4. Arrange tortillas on a working surface.
5. Divide beans mix on each, also add avocado and cashew cheese,
6. Roll burritos and put them in your air fryer.
7. Cover and cook at 300 degrees F for 3 minutes more.
8. Divide burritos between plates and serve!

Day 20: Cinnamon Toast

Servings: 6
Total Time: 15 Minutes
Ingredients And Quantity

- A drizzle of vegetable oil
- 12 vegan bread slices
- ½ cup coconut sugar
- A pinch of black pepper
- 1½ teaspoons vanilla extract
- 1½ teaspoons cinnamon powder

Direction

1. In a bowl, mix oil with cinnamon, sugar, vanilla and a pinch of pepper and stir well.
2. Spread this over bread slices and put them in your air fryer.
3. Cook at 400 degrees F for 5 minutes.
4. Divide them between plates. Serve and enjoy!

Day 21: Baby Carrots And Parsley

Servings: 4
Total Time: 20 Minutes
Ingredients And Quantity
- 2 cups baby carrots
- Salt and black pepper to taste
- 1 tablespoon parsley, chopped
- 1/2 tablespoon olive oil

Direction
1. In a pan that fits your air fryer, mix baby carrots with oil, salt, pepper and parsley.
2. Toss and introduce in your air fryer.
3. Cook at 350 degrees F for 10 minutes.
4. Divide between plates and serve as a side dish.

Day 22: Vegan Chili Fennel

Servings: 4
Total Time: 18 Minutes
Ingredients And Quantity
- 2 fennel bulbs, cut into quarters
- 3 tablespoons olive oil
- Salt and black pepper to taste
- 1 garlic clove, minced
- 1 red chili pepper, chopped
- ¾ cup veggie stock
- Juice of ½ lemon

Direction
1. Heat up a pan that fits your air fryer with the oil over medium-high heat.
2. Add garlic and chili pepper.
3. Stir and cook for 2 minutes.
4. Add fennel, salt, pepper, stock and lemon juice.
5. Toss to coat and introduce in your air fryer.
6. Cook at 350 degrees F for 6 minutes.
7. Divide between plates and serve as a side dish.

Day 23: Collard Greens And Tomatoes

Servings: 4
Total Time: 20 Minutes
Ingredients And Quantity
- 1 pound collard greens
- ¼ cup cherry tomatoes, halved
- 1 tablespoon apple cider vinegar
- 2 tablespoons veggie stock
- Salt and black pepper to the taste

Direction
1. In a pan that fits your air fryer, combine tomatoes, collard greens, vinegar, stock, salt and pepper.
2. Stir and introduce in your air fryer.
3. Cook at 320 degrees F for 10 minutes.
4. Divide between plates and serve as side dish.

Day 24: Savory Tomatoes And Basil Mix

Servings: 2
Total Time: 24 Minutes
Ingredients And Quantity
- 1 bunch basil, chopped
- 3 garlic clove, minced
- A drizzle of olive oil
- Salt and black pepper to taste
- 2 cups cherry tomatoes, halved

Direction
1. In a pan that fits your air fryer, combine tomatoes with garlic, salt, pepper, basil and oil.
2. Toss and introduce in your air fryer.
3. Cook at 320 degrees F for 12 minutes.
4. Divide between plates and serve as a side dish.

Day 25: Mexican Bell Pepper Mix

Servings: 4
Total Time: 26 Minutes
Ingredients And Quantity
- 4 bell peppers, cut into medium chunks
- ½ cup tomato juice
- 2 tablespoons jarred jalapenos, chopped
- 1 cup tomatoes, chopped
- ¼ cup yellow onion, chopped
- ¼ cup green peppers, chopped
- 2 cups tomato sauce
- Salt and black pepper to the taste
- 2 teaspoons onion powder
- ½ teaspoon red pepper, crushed
- 1 teaspoon chili powder
- ½ teaspoons garlic powder
- 1 teaspoon cumin, ground

Direction
1. In a pan that fits your air fryer, mix tomato juice, jalapenos, tomatoes, onion, green peppers, salt, pepper, onion powder, red pepper, chili powder, garlic powder, oregano and cumin.
2. Stir well and introduce in your air fryer.
3. Cook at 350 degrees F for 6 minutes.
4. Add bell peppers and cook at 320 degrees F for another 10 minutes.
5. Divide pepper mix between plates and serve them as side dish.

Day 26: Tasty Broccoli And Mushrooms Mix

Servings: 2
Total Time: 38 Minutes
Ingredients And Quantity

- 10 ounces mushrooms, halved
- 1 broccoli head, florets separated
- 1 garlic clove, minced
- 1 tablespoon balsamic vinegar
- 1 yellow onion, chopped
- 1 tablespoon olive oil
- Salt and black pepper
- 1 teaspoon basil, dried
- 1 avocado, peeled, pitted and roughly cubed
- A pinch of red pepper flakes

Direction

1. In a bowl, mix mushrooms with broccoli, onion, garlic and avocado.
2. In another bowl, mix vinegar, oil, salt, pepper and basil and whisk well.
3. Pour this over veggies and toss to coat.
4. Set aside for 30 minutes.
5. Transfer to your air fryer basket and cook at 350 degrees F for 8 minutes.
6. Divide between plates and serve with pepper flakes on top as a side dish.

Day 27: Red Potatoes And Green Beans

Servings: 4
Total Time: 25 Minutes
Ingredients And Quantity

- 1 pound red potatoes, cut into wedges
- 1 pound green beans
- 2 garlic cloves, minced
- 2 tablespoons olive oil
- Salt and black pepper to taste
- 1/2 teaspoon oregano, dried

Direction

1. In a pan that fits your air fryer, combine potatoes with green beans, garlic, oil, salt, pepper and oregano.
2. Toss and introduce in your air fryer.
3. Cook at 380 degrees F for 15 minutes.
4. Divide between plates and serve as a side dish.

Day 28: Savory Arabic Plum Mix

Servings: 4
Total Time: 22 Minutes
Ingredients And Quantity
- 3 tablespoons stevia
- 3 ounces almonds, peeled and chopped
- 12 ounces plumps, pitted
- 2 tablespoons veggie stock
- 1 teaspoon cumin powder
- 1 teaspoon turmeric powder
- 1 teaspoon ginger powder
- 1 teaspoon cinnamon powder
- 3 tablespoons olive oil
- 2 yellow onions, chopped
- 2 garlic cloves, minced
- Salt and black pepper to taste

Direction
1. In a pan that fits your air fryer, combine almonds with plums, stevia, stock, onions, garlic, salt, pepper, cumin, turmeric, ginger, cinnamon and oil.
2. Toss and introduce in your air fryer.
3. Cook at 350 degrees F for 12 minutes.
4. Divide plum mix between plates. Serve and enjoy!

Day 29: Vegan Portobello Mushrooms

Servings: 4
Total Time: 16 Minutes
Ingredients And Quantity
- 4 big Portobello mushroom caps
- 1 tablespoon olive oil
- 1 cup spinach, torn
- 1/3 cup vegan breadcrumbs
- 1/4 teaspoon rosemary, chopped

Direction
1. Rub mushrooms caps with the oil.
2. Then place them in your air fryer's basket.
3. Cook them at 350 degrees F for 2 minutes.
4. Meanwhile, in a bowl, mix spinach, rosemary and breadcrumbs and stir well.
5. Stuff mushrooms with this mix.
6. Place them in your air fryer's basket again and cook at 350 degrees F for another 10 minutes.
7. Divide them between plates and serve as a side dish.

Day 30: Tasty Broccoli, Tomatoes And Carrots

Servings: 2
Total Time: 24 Minutes
Ingredients And Quantity
- 1 broccoli head, florets separated and steamed
- 1 tomato, chopped
- 3 carrots, chopped and steamed
- 2 ounces soft tofu, crumbled
- 1 teaspoon parsley, chopped
- 1 teaspoon thyme, chopped
- Salt and black pepper to taste

Direction
1. In a pan that fits your air fryer, combine broccoli with tomatoes, carrots, thyme, parsley, salt and pepper.
2. Toss and introduce the air fryer.
3. Cook at 350 degrees F for 10 minutes.
4. Add Tofu and toss again.
5. Introduce in the air fryer and cook for 4 more minutes.
6. Divide between plates. Serve and enjoy!

10 Days Air Fryer Meal Prep Plan For Vegetarians

Day 1: Crunchy Black-Eyed Peas

Servings: 2
Total Time: 10 Minutes
Ingredients And Quantity

- 15 oz. canned black eyed peas, rinsed and drained
- 1/2 tsp. chili powder
- 1/4 tsp. chipotle chili powder
- 1/4 tsp. salt
- Pepper to taste
- Cooking spray

Direction

1. Season the black eyed peas with the chili powder, chipotle chili powder, salt and pepper.
2. Coat the peas with the cooking spray.
3. Preheat the air fryer to 350 degrees F.
4. Cook in the air fryer for 5 minutes.
5. Serve and enjoy!

Day 2: Spiced Crispy Peanuts

Servings: 4
Total Time: 15 Minutes
Ingredients And Quantity

- 2 tsp. rice flour
- 2 tsp. flour
- 1/2 tsp. turmeric powder
- Salt and pepper to taste
- Pinch of baking soda
- 2 cups raw peanuts

Direction

1. Mix the 2 flours, turmeric, red chili, salt, pepper and baking soda.
2. Coat the peanuts with this mixture.
3. Cook the peanuts in the air fryer at 390 degrees F for 10 minutes.
4. Serve and enjoy!

Day 3: Banana Walnut Muffin

Servings: 4
Total Time: 25 Minutes
Ingredients And Quantity

- 1/4 cup powdered sugar
- 1/4 cup unsalted butter
- 1/2 tsp. baking powder
- 1 tsp. milk
- Cooking spray
- 1 tsp. walnuts, chopped
- 1/4 cup banana, mashed
- 1/4 cup oats
- 4 tbsp. flour

Direction

1. Blend the sugar and butter.
2. Add the walnuts and the banana and mix well.
3. In another bowl, combine the oats, flour and baking powder.
4. Combine the mixtures.
5. Pour in the milk to make the consistency thinner.
6. Coat the muffin pan with cooking spray.
7. Air fry the muffin at 160 degrees for 10 minutes.
8. Allow it to cool before serving. Serve and enjoy!

Day 4: Tasty Apricot Pie

Servings: 8
Total Time: 45 Minutes
Ingredients And Quantity

- Juice and zest from ½ lemon
- 4½ oz. brown sugar
- Pich of salt
- 4½ oz. butter
- 9 oz. flour
- 5 tbsp. apricot jam
- 20 oz. raisins
- 7 oz. white sugar
- 1 ½ kg apricot, sliced
- 2 tbsp. vanilla custard
- Pinch of cinnamon

Direction

1. Combine the lemon juice, lemon zest, brown sugar, salt, butter and flour and knead well.
2. In another bowl, put the apricot jam, raisins, white sugar, apricot, vanilla custard and cinnamon.
3. Roll out the dough into a small baking pan.
4. Use a fork to prick holes in the dough.
5. Put the filling on top of the cake.
6. Cook in the air fryer at 320 minutes.
7. Dust with the powdered sugar before serving.
8. Serve and enjoy!

Day 5: Garlic Fries

Servings: 4
Total Time: 1 Hour
Ingredients And Quantity

- 28 oz. potatoes cut into strips
- Water
- Mayo
- 2 tsp. garlic powder
- Cooking spray

Direction

1. Soak the potatoes in water for 30 minutes.
2. Blot dry with a paper towel.
3. Coat the potatoes with garlic powder.
4. Spray with oil.
5. Cook in the air fryer at 360 degrees F for 25 minutes.
6. Serve with the mayo. Enjoy!

Day 6: Lemon Cheesecake

Servings: 8
Total Time: 35 Minutes
Ingredients And Quantity

- Zest and juice from 1 lemon
- 2 tsp. vanilla extract
- 5 oz. sugar
- 17 oz. ricotta
- 3 eggs
- 3 tbsp. cornstarch

Direction

1. Preheat your air fryer to 320 degrees F.
2. In a bowl, mix the lemon zest, lemon juice, vanilla extract, sugar and ricotta.
3. Gradually beat the eggs and stir well.
4. Add the cornstarch and mix well.
5. Pour the mixture into a small oven dish.
6. Place this dish into your air fryer.
7. Cook for 25 minutes.
8. Allow to cool before you serve.
9. Serve and enjoy!

Day 7: Tasty Cranberry Muffin

Servings: 4
Total Time: 25 Minutes
Ingredients And Quantity

- 1 tsp. flour
- 2½ oz. flour
- 1½ tsp. baking powder
- Pinch of salt
- 3 tbsp. sugar
- 1 egg
- 75 ml milk
- 2½ dried cranberries
- 1½ oz. butter, melted

Direction

1. Preheat your air fryer to 390 degrees F.
2. Blend the cinnamon, flour, baking powder, salt and sugar in a bowl.
3. In a separate bowl, beat the egg.
4. Gradually add the milk, cranberries and butter.
5. Pour the batter into a muffin pan.
6. Now cook in the air fryer for 15 minutes or until it turns golden.
7. Serve and enjoy!

Day 8: Broccoli Salad With Goat Cheese

Servings: 5
Total Time: 45 Minutes
Ingredients And Quantity

- 2 oz. broccoli florets
- 4 bell peppers, sliced
- 3 onions, chopped
- Cooking spray
- Salt and pepper to taste
- 3½ oz. goat cheese
- 4 tomatoes, sliced

Direction

1. Coat the broccoli bell peppers and onions with cooking spray.
2. Air fry at 360 degrees F for 10 minutes.
3. Transfer the broccoli mixture to a salad bowl.
4. Top with the goat cheese and tomatoes.
5. Season with the salt and pepper.
6. Serve and enjoy!

Day 9: Veggie And Pasta Salad

Servings: 16
Total Time: 1 Hour 25 Minutes
Ingredients And Quantity

- 3 eggplants, sliced into thick rounds
- 3 zucchinis, sliced
- 2 tbsp. olive oil, divided
- 4 tomatoes, sliced
- 2 red bell peppers, sliced
- 8 cups cooked elbow pasta
- 1/2 cup fresh basil leaves, chopped
- 1/2 cup low fat Italian dressing
- 2 tsp. salt
- 8 tbsp. Parmesan cheese, grated

Direction

1. Coat the eggplants and zucchinis with half of the oil.
2. Roast in the air fryer at 360 degrees F for 30 minutes.
3. Remove from the air fryer.
4. Coat the tomatoes and red bell peppers with the remaining oil.
5. Cook in the air fryer for 10 minutes.
6. Put the pasta in a bowl.
7. Toss with the roasted vegetables and fresh basil.
8. Drizzle with the dressing.
9. Season with the salt and Parmesan.
10. Chill in the refrigerator before serving.
11. Serve and enjoy!

Day 10: Broccoli Fried Cutlets With Chickpeas

Servings: 2
Total Time: 30 Minutes
Ingredients And Quantity

- 1/2 cup chickpeas, soaked and cooked in a pressure cooker
- 1/2 cup broccoli florets
- Hot water
- 1 onion, chopped
- Salt to taste
- 1 tsp. green chili, chopped
- 1 tbsp. lemon juice
- 1/4 tsp. cumin
- 1/4 tsp. coriander powder

Direction

1. Put the chickpeas in a food processor.
2. Pulse until it becomes a paste.
3. Soak the broccoli florets in boiling water.
4. Drain the water.
5. Grate and combine with the chickpeas.
6. Now add the rest of the ingredients.
7. Form round patties from the mixture.
8. Cook in the air fryer at 360 degrees F for 10 minutes.
9. Flip and cook the other side for 5 minutes.
10. Serve and enjoy!